THE
NARCOTICS ANONYMOUS
STEP WORKING GUIDES

THE
NARCOTICS ANONYMOUS
STEP WORKING GUIDES

Narcotics Anonymous World Services, Inc.
Chatsworth, California

World Service Office
PO Box 9999
Van Nuys, CA 91409
Tel. (818) 773-9999
Fax (818) 700-0700
Website: www.na.org

World Service Office–EUROPE
48 Rue de l' Eté
B-1050 Brussels, Belgium
Tel. +32/2/646-6012
Fax +32/2/649-9239

World Service Office–CANADA
150 Britannia Rd. E. Unit 21
Mississauga, Ontario, L4Z 2A4, Canada
Tel. (905) 507-0100
Fax (905) 507-0101

ISBN 1-55776-370-4   English   10/03

WSO Catalog Item No. EN-1400

Table of Contents

PREFACE

The idea for this piece of literature came from the Narcotics Anonymous Fellowship itself. Beginning in the early 1980s, we began receiving Twelve Step guides and step worksheets along with requests that we develop a standard set of guides for the NA Fellowship to use in working through the Twelve Steps. Fellowship demand propelled this project up the NA World Service Conference Literature Committee's priority worklists, and finally resulted in the World Service Conference directing the WSCLC to go ahead with the project at WSC'95.

The working title for this project for many years was the "Step Writing Guides." However, we recognized that the word "writing" imposed a limitation on members who may be unable to write or may choose not to use writing as the means for working the Twelve Steps. Therefore, the title became the *Step Working Guides*.

Each chapter includes both narrative and questions. The narrative is meant to provoke thought about the questions, but is not meant to be comprehensive. There is a difference in "voice" between the narrative and the questions. The narrative is written in the "we" voice in order to promote unity about what we all have in common: our addiction and recovery. The questions are written in the individual "I" voice so that each member using these guides can personalize the work. The *Step Working Guides* is a companion piece to *It Works: How and Why*. Thorough discussion of each of the Twelve Steps is contained in that work. Additional information about NA recovery can be found in other NA literature. If we find that any of the terms used in this book are unfamiliar, we should feel free to make use of a dictionary.

These guides are meant to be used by NA members at any stage of recovery, whether it's our first time through the steps or we've been living with the steps as our guiding force for many years. This book is intentionally written to be relevant to newcomers and to help more experienced members develop a deeper understanding of the Twelve Steps. As NA grows in numbers, in diversity, and in strength and longevity of clean time, we need literature that will continue to serve the needs of the fellowship, literature that "grows" along with the fellowship.

However, as open and inclusive as we tried to be when writing these guides, we realized that we would never be able to write something that captured every member's experience with the steps. In fact, we wouldn't have tried to do that, even if we thought it were possible. This book contains guides to working the Twelve Steps toward recovery; it does not contain recovery itself. Recovery is ultimately found in each member's personal experience with working the steps. You can add to these guides, delete from them, or use them as they are. It's your choice.

There's probably only one inappropriate way to use these guides: alone. We can't overemphasize the importance of working with a sponsor in working the steps. In fact, in our fellowship, a sponsor is considered, first and foremost, a guide through the Twelve

Steps. If you haven't yet asked someone to sponsor you, please do so before beginning these guides.

Merely reading all the available information about any of the Twelve Steps will never be sufficient to bring about a true change in our lives and freedom from our disease. It's our goal to make the steps part of who we are. To do that, we have to work them. Hence, the *Step Working Guides*.

Like every piece of NA literature, this was written by addicts for addicts. We hope that every member who uses this book will be encouraged and inspired. We are grateful to have been given the opportunity to participate in this project. Thank you for allowing us to be of service.

WSC Literature Committee

"We admitt_ed_ that _we_ _were_ powerless over our addiction, that our lives had become unmanageable."

—Step One

A "first" of anything is a beginning, and so it is with the steps: The First Step is the beginning of the recovery process. The healing starts here; we can't go any further until we've worked this step.

Some NA members "feel" their way through the First Step, by intuition; others choose to work Step One in a more systematic fashion. Our reasons for formally working Step One will vary from member to member. It may be that we're new to recovery, and we've just fought—and lost—an exhausting battle with drugs. It may be that we've been around awhile, abstinent from drugs, but we've discovered that our disease has become active in some other area of our lives, forcing us to face our powerlessness and the unmanageability of our lives once again. Not every act of growth is motivated by pain; it may just be time to cycle through the steps again, thus beginning the next stage of our never-ending journey of recovery.

Some of us find a measure of comfort in realizing that a *disease*, not a moral failing, has caused us to reach this bottom. Others don't really care what the cause has been— we just want out!

Whatever the case, it's time to do some step work: to engage in some concrete activity that will help us find more freedom from our addiction, whatever shape it is currently taking. Our hope is to internalize the principles of Step One, to deepen our surrender, to make the principles of acceptance, humility, willingness, honesty, and open-mindedness a fundamental part of who we are.

First, we must arrive at a point of surrender. There are many different ways to do this. For some of us, the road we traveled getting to the First Step was more than enough to convince us that unconditional surrender was our only option. Others of us start this process even though we're not entirely convinced that we're addicts or that we've really hit bottom. Only in working the First Step do we truly come to realize that we *are* addicts, that we *have* hit bottom, and that we must surrender.

Before we begin working the First Step, we must become abstinent—whatever it takes. If we're new in Narcotics Anonymous and our First Step is primarily about looking at the effects of drug addiction in our lives, we need to get clean. If we've been clean awhile and our First Step is about our powerlessness over some other behavior that's made our lives unmanageable, we need to find a way to stop the behavior so that our surrender isn't clouded by continued acting out.

The Disease of Addiction

What makes us addicts is the disease of addiction—not the drugs, not our behavior, but our disease. There is something within us that makes us unable to control our use of drugs. This same "something" also makes us prone to obsession and compulsion in other areas of our lives. How can we tell when our disease is active? When we become trapped in obsessive, compulsive, self-centered routines, endless loops that lead no-where but to physical, mental, spiritual, and emotional decay.

1 • What does "the disease of addiction" mean to me?

2 • Has my disease been active recently? In what way?

3 • What is it like when I'm obsessed with something? Does my thinking follow a pattern? Describe.

4 • When a thought occurs to me, do I immediately act on it without considering the consequences? In what other ways do I behave compulsively?

5 • How does the self-centered part of my disease affect my life and the lives of those around me?

6 • How has my disease affected me physically? Mentally? Spiritually? Emotionally?

Our addiction can manifest itself in a variety of ways. When we first come to Narcotics Anonymous, our problem will, of course, be drugs. Later on, we may find out that addiction is wreaking havoc in our lives in any number of ways.

7 • What is the specific way in which my addiction has been manifesting itself most recently?

8 • Have I been obsessed with a person, place, or thing? If so, how has that gotten in the way of my relationships with others? How else have I been affected mentally, physically, spiritually, and emotionally by this obsession?

Denial

Denial is the part of our disease that tells us we don't have a disease. When we are in denial, we are unable to see the reality of our addiction. We minimize its effect. We blame others, citing the too-high expectations of families, friends, employers. We com-pare ourselves with other addicts whose addiction seems "worse" than our own. We may blame one particular drug. If we have been abstinent from drugs for some time, we might compare the current manifestation of our addiction with our drug use, rationaliz-ing that nothing we do today could possibly be as bad as *that* was! One of the easiest ways to tell that we are in denial is when we find ourselves giving plausible but untrue reasons for our behavior.

9 • Have I given plausible but untrue reasons for my behavior? What have they been?

10 • Have I compulsively acted on an obsession, and then acted as if I had actually *planned* to act that way? When were those times?

11 • How have I blamed other people for my behavior?

12 • How have I compared my addiction with others' addiction? Is my addiction "bad enough" if I don't compare it to anyone else's?

13 • Am I comparing a current manifestation of my addiction to the way my life was before I got clean? Am I plagued by the idea that I should know better?

14 • Have I been thinking that I have enough information about addiction and recovery to get my behavior under control before it gets out of hand?

15 • Am I avoiding action because I'm afraid I will be ashamed when I face the results of my addiction? Am I avoiding action because I'm worried about what others will think?

Hitting bottom: Despair and Isolation

Our addiction finally brings us to a place where we can no longer deny the nature of our problem. All the lies, all the rationalizations, all the illusions fall away as we stand face-to-face with what our lives have become. We realize we've been living without hope. We find we've become friendless or so completely disconnected that our relationships are a sham, a parody of love and intimacy. Though it may seem that all is lost when we find ourselves in this state, the truth is that we must pass through this place before we can embark upon our journey of recovery.

16 • What crisis brought me to recovery?

17 • What situation led me to formally work Step One?

18 • When did I first recognize my addiction as a problem? Did I try to correct it? If so, how? If not, why not?

Powerlessness

As addicts, we react to the word "powerless" in a variety of ways. Some of us recognize that a more accurate description of our situation simply could not exist, and admit our powerlessness with a sense of relief. Others recoil at the word, connecting it with weakness or believing it to indicate some kind of character deficiency. Understanding powerlessness—and how admitting our own powerlessness is essential to our recovery—will help us get over any negative feelings we may have about the concept.

We are powerless when the driving force in our life is beyond our control. Our addiction certainly qualifies as such an uncontrollable, driving force. We cannot moderate or control our drug use or other compulsive behaviors, even when they are causing us to lose the things that matter most to us. We cannot stop, even when to continue will surely result in irreparable physical damage. We find ourselves doing things that we would never do if it weren't for our addiction, things that make us shudder with shame when we think of them. We may even decide that we don't want to use, that we aren't going to use, and realize we are simply unable to stop when the opportunity presents itself.

We may have tried to abstain from drug use or other compulsive behaviors—perhaps with some success—for a period of time without a program, only to find that our untreated addiction eventually takes us right back to where we were before. In order to work the First Step, we need to prove our own individual powerlessness to ourselves on a deep level.

19 • Over what, exactly, am I powerless?

20 • I've done things while acting out on my addiction that I would never do when focusing on recovery. What were they?

21 • What things have I done to maintain my addiction that went completely against all my beliefs and values?

22 • How does my personality change when I'm acting out on my addiction? (For example: Do I become arrogant? Self-centered? Mean-tempered? Passive to the point where I can't protect myself? Manipulative? Whiny?)

23 • Do I manipulate other people to maintain my addiction? How?

24 • Have I tried to quit using and found that I couldn't? Have I quit using on my own and found that my life was so painful without drugs that my abstinence didn't last very long? What were these times like?

25 • How has my addiction caused me to hurt myself or others?

Unmanageability

The First Step asks us to admit two things: one, that we are powerless over our addiction; and two, that our lives have become unmanageable. Actually, we would be hard pressed to admit one and not the other. Our unmanageability is the outward evidence of our powerlessness. There are two general types of unmanageability: outward unmanageability, the kind that can be seen by others; and inner, or personal, unmanageability.

Outward unmanageability is often identified by such things as arrests, job losses, and family problems. Some of our members have been incarcerated. Some have never been able to sustain any kind of relationship for more than a few months. Some of us have been cut off from our families, asked never again to contact them.

Inner or personal unmanageability is often identified by unhealthy or untrue belief systems about ourselves, the world we live in, and the people in our lives. We may believe we're worthless. We may believe that the world revolves around us—not just that it *should*, but that it *does*. We may believe that it isn't really our job to take care of ourselves; someone else should do that. We may believe that the responsibilities the average person takes on as a matter of course are just too large a burden for us to bear. We may over or under react to events in our lives. Emotional volatility is often one of the most obvious ways in which we can identify personal unmanageability.

25 • What does unmanageability mean to me?

26 • Have I ever been arrested or had legal trouble as a result of my addiction? Have I ever done anything I could have been arrested for if only I were caught? What have those things been?

4

27 • What trouble have I had at work or school because of my addiction?

8 • What trouble have I had with my family as a result of my addiction?

9 • What trouble have I had with my friends as a result of my addiction?

30 • Do I insist on having my own way? What effect has my insistence had on my relationships?

31 • Do I consider the needs of others? What effect has my lack of consideration had on my relationships?

32 • Do I accept responsibility for my life and my actions? Am I able to carry out my daily responsibilities without becoming overwhelmed? How has this affected my life?

33 • Do I fall apart the minute things don't go according to plan? How has this affected my life?

34 • Do I treat every challenge as a personal insult? How has this affected my life?

35 • Do I maintain a crisis mentality, responding to every situation with panic? How has this affected my life?

36 • Do I ignore signs that something may be seriously wrong with my health or with my children, thinking things will work out somehow? Describe.

37 • When in real danger, have I ever been either indifferent to that danger or somehow unable to protect myself as a result of my addiction? Describe.

38 • Have I ever harmed someone as a result of my addiction? Describe.

39 • Do I have temper tantrums or react to my feelings in other ways that lower my self-respect or sense of dignity? Describe.

40 • Did I take drugs or act out on my addiction to change or suppress my feelings? What was I trying to change or suppress?

Reservations

Reservations are places in our program that we have *reserved* for relapse. They may be built around the idea that we can retain a small measure of control, something like, "Okay, I accept that I can't control my using, but I can still sell drugs, can't I?" Or we may think we can remain friends with the people we used with or bought drugs from. We may think that certain parts of the program don't apply to us. We may think there's some- thing we just can't face clean—a serious illness, for instance, or the death of a loved one—and plan to use if it ever happens. We may think that after we've accomplished some goal, made a certain amount of money, or been clean for a certain number of years, *then* we'll be able to control our using. Reservations are usually tucked away in the back of our minds; we are not fully conscious of them. It is essential that we expose any reservations we may have and cancel them—right here, right now.

41 • Have I accepted the full measure of my disease?

42. • Do I think I can still associate with the people connected with my addiction? Can I still go to the places where I used? Do I think it's wise to keep drugs or paraphernalia around, just to "remind myself" or test my recovery? If so, why?

43. • Is there something I think I can't get through clean, some event that might happen that will be so painful that I'll have to use to survive the hurt?

44. • Do I think that with some amount of clean time, or with different life circumstances, I'd be able to control my using?

45. • What reservations am I still holding on to?

Surrender

There's a huge difference between resignation and surrender. Resignation is what we feel when we've realized we're addicts but haven't yet accepted recovery as the solution to our problem. Many of us found ourselves at this point long before coming to Narcotics Anonymous. We may have thought that it was our destiny to be addicts, to live and die in our addiction. Surrender, on the other hand, is what happens after we've accepted the First Step as something that is true for us *and* have accepted that recovery is the solution. We don't want our lives to be the way they have been. We don't want to keep feeling the way we've been feeling.

46 • What am I afraid of about the concept of surrender, if anything?

47 • What convinces me that I can't use successfully anymore?

48 • Do I accept that I'll never regain control, even after a long period of abstinence?

49 • Can I begin my recovery without a complete surrender?

50 • What would my life be like if I surrendered completely?

51 • Can I continue my recovery without complete surrender?

Spiritual Principles

In the First Step, we will focus on honesty, open-mindedness, willingness, humility, and acceptance. The practice of the principle of honesty from the First Step starts with admitting the truth about our addiction, and continues with the practice of honesty on a daily basis. When we say "I'm an addict" in a meeting, it may be the first truly honest thing we've said in a long time. We begin to be able to be honest with ourselves and, consequently, with other people.

52 • If I've been thinking about using or acting out on my addiction in some other way, have I shared it with my sponsor or told anyone else?

53 • Have I stayed in touch with the reality of my disease, no matter how long I've had freedom from active addiction?

54 • Have I noticed that, now that I don't have to cover up my addiction, I no longer need to lie like I did? Do I appreciate the freedom that goes along with that? In what ways have I begun to be honest in my recovery?

Practicing the principle of open-mindedness found in Step One mostly involves being ready to believe that there might be another way to live and being willing to try that way. It doesn't matter that we can't see every detail of what that way might be, or that it may be totally unlike anything we've heard about before; what matters is that we don't limit ourselves or our thinking. Sometimes we may hear NA members saying things that sound totally crazy to us, things like "surrender to win" or suggestions to pray for someone we resent. We demonstrate open-mindedness when we don't reject these things without having tried them.

55 • What have I heard in recovery that I have trouble believing? Have I asked my sponsor, or the person I heard say it, to explain it to me?

56 • In what ways am I practicing open-mindedness?

The principle of willingness contained in the First Step can be practiced in a variety of ways. When we first begin to think about recovery, many of us either don't really believe it's possible for us or just don't understand how it will work, but we go ahead with the First Step anyway—and that's our first experience with willingness. Taking any action that will help our recovery shows willingness: going to meetings early and staying late, helping set up meetings, getting other NA members' phone numbers and calling them.

57 • Am I willing to follow my sponsor's direction?

58 • Am I willing to go to meetings regularly?

59 • Am I willing to give recovery my best effort? In what ways?

The principle of humility, so central to the First Step, is expressed most purely in our surrender. Humility is most easily identified as an acceptance of who we truly are—neither worse nor better than we believed we were when we were using, just *human*.

60 • Do I believe that I'm a monster who has poisoned the whole world with my addiction? Do I believe that my addiction is utterly inconsequential to the larger society around me? Or something in between?

61 • Do I have a sense of my relative importance within my circle of family and friends? In society as whole? What is that sense?

62 • How am I practicing the principle of humility in connection with this work on the First Step?

To practice the principle of acceptance, we must do more than merely admit that we're addicts. When we accept our addiction, we feel a profound inner change that is underscored by a rising sense of hope. We also begin to feel a sense of peace. We come to terms with our addiction, with our recovery, and with the meaning those two realities will come to have in our lives. We don't dread a future of meeting attendance, sponsor contact, and step work; instead, we begin to see recovery as a precious gift, and the work connected with it as no more trouble than other routines of life.

- Have I made peace with the fact that I'm an addict?
- Have I made peace with the things I'll have to do to stay clean?
- How is acceptance of my disease necessary for my continued recovery?

Moving on

As we get ready to go on to Step Two, we'll probably find ourselves wondering if we've worked Step One well enough. Are we sure it's time to move on? Have we spent as much time as others may have spent on this step? Have we truly gained an understanding of this step? Many of us have found it helpful to write about our understanding of each step as we prepare to move on.

- How do I know it's time to move on?
- What is my understanding of Step One?
- How has my prior knowledge and experience affected my work on this step?

We've come to a place where we see the results of our old way of life and accept that a new way is called for, but we probably don't yet see how rich with possibilities the life of recovery is. It may be enough just to have freedom from active addiction right now, but we will soon find that the void we have been filling with drugs or other obsessive and compulsive behaviors begs to be filled. Working the rest of the steps will fill that void. Next on our journey toward recovery is Step Two.

"We <u>came</u> to believe that a Power greater than ourselves could restore us to sanity."

—Step Two

Step One strips us of our illusions about addiction; Step Two gives us hope for recovery. The Second Step tells us that what we found out about our addiction in the First Step is not the end of the story. The pain and insanity with which we have been living are unnecessary, says Step Two. They can be relieved and, in time, we will learn to live without them through working the Twelve Steps of Narcotics Anonymous.

The Second Step fills the void we feel when we've finished Step One. As we approach Step Two, we begin to consider that maybe, just maybe, there's a Power greater than ourselves—a Power capable of healing our hurt, calming our confusion, and restoring our sanity.

When we were new in the program, many of us were puzzled by this step's implication that we had been insane. From acknowledging our powerlessness to admitting our "insanity" seemed an awfully large leap. However, after being around the program for a while, we began to understand what this step was really about. We read the Basic Text and found that our insanity was defined there as "repeating the same mistakes and expecting different results." We could certainly relate to *that*! After all, how many times had we tried to get away with something we had *never* gotten away with before, each time telling ourselves, "It will be different this time?" Now, that's insane! As we live the principles of this step for many years, we discover how deep our insanity actually runs; we often find that the Basic Text definition just scratches the surface.

Some of us resisted this step because we thought it required us to be religious. Nothing could be further from the truth. There is nothing, absolutely nothing, in the NA program that requires a member to be religious. The idea that "anyone may join us, regardless of … religion or lack of religion" is fiercely defended by our fellowship. Our members strive to be inclusive in this regard and do not tolerate anything that compromises the unconditional right of all addicts to develop their own individual understanding of a Power greater than themselves. This is a spiritual, not religious, program.

The beauty of the Second Step is revealed when we begin to think about what our Higher Power can be. We are encouraged to choose a Power that is loving, caring, and—most importantly—able to restore us to sanity. The Second Step does not say, "We came to believe *in* a Power greater than ourselves." It says, "We came to believe *that* a Power greater than ourselves *could restore us to sanity*." The emphasis is not on who or what this Power is, but on what this Power can do for us. The group itself certainly qualifies as a Power greater than ourselves. So do the spiritual principles contained in the Twelve Steps. And, of course, so does the understanding any one of our individual members has of a Higher Power. As we stay clean and continue to work this step, we discover that no matter how long our addiction has gone on and how far our insanity has progressed, there's no limit to the ability of a Power greater than ourselves to restore our sanity.

Hope

The hope we get from working Step Two replaces the desperation with which we came into the program. Every time we had followed what we'd thought would be a path out of our addiction—medicine, religion, or psychiatry, for instance—we found they only took us so far; none of these was sufficient for us. As we ran out of options and exhausted our resources, we wondered if we'd ever find a solution to our dilemma, if there was anything in the world that *worked*. In fact, we may have been slightly suspicious when we first came to Narcotics Anonymous, wondering if this was just another method that wouldn't work, or that wouldn't work well enough for us to make a difference.

However, something remarkable occurred to us as we sat in our first few meetings. There were other addicts there who had used drugs just as we had, addicts who were now clean. We believed in them. We knew we could trust them. They knew the places we'd been to in our addiction—not just the using hangouts, not just the geographic locations, but the hangouts of horror and despair our spirits had visited each time we'd used. The recovering addicts we met in NA knew those places as well as we did because they had been there themselves.

It was when we realized that these other members—addicts like ourselves—were staying clean and finding freedom that most of us first experienced the feeling of hope. We may have been standing with a group of members after a meeting. We may have been listening to someone share a story just like our own. Most of us can recall that moment, even years later—and that moment comes to all of us.

Our hope is renewed throughout our recovery. Each time something new is revealed to us about our disease, the pain of that realization is accompanied by a surge of hope. No matter how painful the process of demolishing our denial may be, something else is being restored in its place within us. Even if we don't feel like we believe in anything, we do believe in the program. We believe that we can be restored to sanity, even in the most hopeless times, even in our sickest areas.

 • What do I have hope about today?

Insanity

If we have any doubts about the need for a renewal of sanity in our lives, we're going to have trouble with this step. Reviewing our First Step should help us if we're having doubts. Now is the time to take a good look at our insanity.

 • Did I believe I could control my using? What were some of my experiences with this, and how were my efforts unsuccessful?

 • What things did I do that I can hardly believe I did when I look back at them? Did I put myself in dangerous situations to get drugs? Did I behave in ways of which I'm now ashamed? What were those situations like?

4 ~~7~~ • Did I make insane decisions as a result of my addiction?
Did I quit jobs, leave friendships and other relationships, or give up on achieving other goals for no reason other than that those things interfered with my using?

5 ~~4~~ • Did I ever physically injure myself or someone else in my addiction?

Insanity is a loss of our perspective and our sense of proportion. For example, we may think that our personal problems are more important than anyone else's; in fact, we may not even be able to consider other people's needs at all. Small problems become major catastrophes. Our lives get out of balance. Some obvious examples of insane thinking are the belief that we can stay clean on our own, or the belief that using drugs was our only problem and that everything is fine now just because we're clean. In Narcotics Anonymous, insanity is often described as the belief that we can take something *outside* ourselves—drugs, power, sex, food—to fix what's wrong *inside* ourselves: our feelings.

6 ~~5~~ • How have I overreacted or underreacted to things?

7 ~~6~~ • How has my life been out of balance?

8 ~~7~~ • In what ways does my insanity tell me that things outside myself can make me whole or solve all my problems? Using drugs? Compulsive gambling, eating, or sex seeking? Something else?

9 ~~8~~ • Is part of my insanity the belief that the symptom of my addiction (using drugs or some other manifestation) is my only problem?

If we've been clean for a while, we may find that a whole new level of denial is making it difficult to see the insanity in our lives. Just as we did in the beginning of our recovery, we need to become familiar with the ways in which we have been insane. Many of us have found that our understanding of insanity goes further than the definition of insanity in the Basic Text. We make the same mistakes over and over again, even when we're fully aware of what the results will be. Perhaps we're hurting so bad that we don't care about the consequences, or we figure that acting on an obsession will somehow be worth the price.

• When we've acted on an obsession, even though we knew what the results would be, what were we feeling and thinking beforehand? What made us go ahead?

Coming to Believe

The discussion above provides several reasons why we may have trouble with this step. There may be others. It's important for us to identify and overcome any barriers that could prevent us from coming to believe.

10 ~~9~~ • Do I have any fears about coming to believe? What are they?

11 ~~10~~ • Do I have any other barriers that make it difficult for me to believe? What are they?

12 ~~11~~ • What does the phrase "We came to believe…" mean to me?

13

As addicts, we're prone to wanting everything to happen instantly. But it's important to remember that Step Two is a process, not an event. Most of us don't just wake up one day and know that a Power greater than ourselves can restore us to sanity. We gradually grow into this belief. Still, we don't have to just sit back and wait for our belief to grow on its own; we can help it along.

13 • Have I ever believed in anything for which I didn't have tangible evidence? What was that experience like?

14 • What experiences have I heard other recovering addicts share about the process of coming to believe? Have I tried any of them in my life?

15 • In what do I believe?

16 • How has my belief grown since I've been in recovery?

A Power Greater than Ourselves

Each one us comes to recovery with a whole history of life experiences. That history will determine to a large degree the kind of understanding we develop of a Power greater than ourselves. In this step, we don't have to have a lot of specific ideas about the nature or identity of that Higher Power. That sort of understanding will come later. The kind of understanding of a Higher Power that's most important to find in the Second Step is an understanding that can *help* us. We're not concerned here with theological elegance or doctrinal adherence—we just want something that *works*.

How powerful does a Power greater than ourselves have to be? The answer to that question is simple. Our addiction as a negative power was, without a doubt, greater than we were. Our addiction led us down a path of insanity and caused us to act differently than we wanted to behave. We need something to combat that, something at least as powerful as our addiction.

17 • Do I have problems accepting that there is a Power or Powers greater than myself?

18 • What are some things that are more powerful than I am?

19 • Can a Power greater than myself help me stay clean? How?

20 • Can a Power greater than I am help me recover? How?

Some of us may have a very clear idea about the nature of a Power greater than ourselves, and there's absolutely nothing wrong with that. In fact, Step Two is the point at which many of us begin to form our first practical ideas about a Power greater than ourselves, if we haven't already. Many addicts have found it helpful to identify what a Power greater than ourselves is *not* before identifying what it *is*. In addition, looking at what a Power greater than ourselves can do for us may help us begin to discover more about that Power.

There are many, many understandings of a Power greater than ourselves that we can develop. We can think of it as the power of spiritual principles, the power of the NA Fellowship, "good orderly direction," or anything else of which we can conceive, as long as it is loving and caring and more powerful than we are. As a matter of fact, we don't have to have any *understanding* at all of a Power greater than ourselves to be able to use that Power to stay clean and seek recovery.

20 • What evidence do I have that a Higher Power is working in my life?

21 • What are the characteristics my Higher Power does *not* have?

22 • What are the characteristics my Higher Power has?

Restoration to Sanity

It Works: How and Why defines the term "restoration" as "changing to a point where addiction and its accompanying insanity are not controlling our lives." We find that just as our insanity was evident in our loss of perspective and sense of proportion, so we can see sanity in our lives when we begin developing a perspective that allows us to make better decisions. We find that we have choices about how to act. We begin to have the maturity and wisdom to slow down and consider all aspects of a situation before acting.

Naturally, our lives will change. Most of us have no trouble identifying the sanity in our lives when we compare our using with our early recovery, our early recovery with some time clean, and some time clean with long-term recovery. All of this is a process, and our need for a restoration to sanity will change over time.

When we're new in the program, being restored to sanity probably means not having to use anymore; when that happens, perhaps some of the insanity that is directly and obviously tied to our using will stop. We'll quit committing crimes to get drugs. We'll cease putting ourselves in certain degrading situations that serve no purpose but our using.

If we've been in recovery for some time, we may find that we have no trouble believing in a Power greater than ourselves that can help us stay clean, but we may not have considered what a restoration to sanity means to us beyond staying clean. As we grow in our recovery, it's very important that our idea of the meaning of "sanity" also grows.

23 • What are some things I consider examples of sanity?

24 • What changes in my thinking and behavior are necessary for my restoration to sanity?

25 • In what areas of my life do I need sanity now?

26 • How is restoration a process?

27 • How will working the rest of the steps help me in my restoration to sanity?

28 • How has sanity already been restored to me in my recovery?

Some of us may have unrealistic expectations about being restored to sanity. We may think that we'll never get angry again or that, as soon as we start to work this step, we will behave perfectly all the time and have no more trouble with obsessions, emotional turmoil, or imbalance in our lives. This description may seem extreme, but if we find ourselves disappointed with our personal growth in recovery or the amount of time it takes to be "restored to sanity," we may recognize some of our beliefs in this description. Most of us have found that we gain the most serenity by letting go of *any* expectations we may have about how our recovery is progressing.

30 • What expectations do I have about being restored to sanity? Are they realistic or unrealistic?

31 • Are my realistic expectations about how my recovery is progressing being met or not? Do I understand that recovery happens over time, not overnight?

32 • Finding ourselves able to act sanely, even once, in a situation with which we were never able to deal successfully before is evidence of sanity. Have I had any experiences like that in my recovery? What were they?

Spiritual Principles

In the Second Step, we will focus on open-mindedness, willingness, faith, trust, and humility. The principle of open-mindedness that we find in the Second Step arises from the understanding that we can't recover alone, that we need some kind of help. It continues with opening our minds to believing that help is possible for us. It doesn't matter whether we have any idea of how this Power greater than ourselves is going to help, just that we believe it's possible.

33 • Why is having a closed mind harmful to my recovery?

34 • How am I demonstrating open-mindedness in my life today?

35 • In what ways has my life changed since I've been in recovery? Do I believe more change is possible?

Practicing the principle of willingness in the Second Step may begin simply. At first we may just go to meetings and listen to other recovering addicts share about their experiences with this step. Then we may begin applying what we hear to our own recovery. Of course, we ask our sponsor to guide us.

36 • What am I willing to do to be restored to sanity?

37 • Is there something I am now willing to do that I was previously unwilling to do? What is it?

We can't just sit back and wait to feel a sense of faith when working Step Two. We have to work at it. One of the suggestions that has worked for many of us is to "act as if" we had faith. This doesn't mean that we should be dishonest with ourselves. We don't need to lie to our sponsor or anyone else about where we are with this step. We're not doing this to sound good or look good. "Acting as if" simply means living as though we believe that what we hope for will happen. In the Second Step, this would mean living as though we expect to be restored to sanity. There are a variety of ways this may work in our individual lives. Many members suggest that we can begin "acting as if" by going to meetings regularly and taking direction from our sponsor.

38 • What action have I been taking that demonstrates my faith?

39 • How has my faith grown?

40 • Have I been able to make plans, having faith that my addiction isn't going to get in the way?

Practicing the principle of trust may require overcoming a sense of fear about the process of being restored to sanity. Even if we've been clean only a short time, we've probably already experienced some emotional pain as we've grown in recovery. We may be afraid that there will be more pain. In one sense, we're right about this: There *will* be more pain. None of it, however, will be more than we can bear, and none of it has to be borne alone. If we can develop our sense of trust in the process of recovery and in a Power greater than ourselves, we can walk through the painful times in our recovery. We'll know that what's waiting on the other side will be more than just superficial happiness; it will be a fundamental transformation that will make our lives more satisfying on a deeper level.

41 • What fears do I have that are getting in the way of my trust?

42 • What do I need to do to let go of these fears?

43 • What action am I taking that demonstrates my trust in the process of recovery and a Power greater than myself?

The principle of humility springs from our acknowledgment that there *is* a Power greater than ourselves. It's a tremendous struggle for most of us to stop relying on our own thinking and begin to ask for help, but when we do, we have begun to practice the principle of humility found in the Second Step.

44 • Have I sought help from a Power greater than myself today? How?

45 • Have I sought help from my sponsor, gone to meetings, and reached out to other recovering addicts? What were the results?

Moving on

As we get ready to go on to Step Three, we'll want to take a look at what we've gained by working Step Two. Writing about our understanding of each step as we prepare to move on helps us internalize the spiritual principles connected to it.

46. • What action can I take that will help me along in the process of coming to believe?

47. • What am I doing to work on overcoming any unrealistic expectations I may have about being restored to sanity?

48. • What is my understanding of Step Two?

49. • How has my prior knowledge and experience affected my work on this step?

As we move on to Step Three, a sense of hope is probably arising within our spirits. Even if we're not new in recovery, we've just reinforced our knowledge that recovery, growth, and change are not just possible but inevitable when we make the effort to work the steps. We can see the possibility of relief from the particular brand of insanity in which we've most recently been gripped by our addiction. We've probably already begun to experience some freedom. We're beginning to be released from the blind pursuit of our insanity. We've explored our insanity and have started to trust a Power greater than ourselves to relieve us from having to continue on the same path. We're beginning to be freed from our illusions. We no longer have to struggle to keep our addiction a secret or isolate ourselves to hide our insanity. We have seen how the program has worked for others, and we have discovered that it is beginning to work for us as well. Through our newfound faith, we achieve the willingness to move into action and work Step Three.

"We made a decision to turn our will and our lives over to the care of God as we understood Him."

—Step Three

We've worked Steps One and Two with our sponsor—we've surrendered, and we've demonstrated our willingness to try something new. This has charged us with a strong sense of hope. But if we do not translate our hope into action right now, it will fade away, and we'll end up right back where we started. The action we need to take is working Step Three.

The central action in Step Three is a decision. The idea of making that decision may terrify us, especially when we look at what we're deciding to do in this step. Making a decision, any decision, is something most of us haven't done in a long time. We've had our decisions made for us—by our addiction, by the authorities, or just by default because we didn't want the responsibility of deciding anything for ourselves. When we add to this the concept of entrusting the care of our will and our lives to something that most of us *don't* understand at this point, we may just think this whole thing is beyond us and start looking for a shortcut or an easier way to work our programs. These thoughts are dangerous, for when we take shortcuts in our program, we short-circuit our recovery.

The Third Step decision may be too big to make in one leap. Our fears of the Third Step, and the dangerous thinking to which those fears lead, can be eased by breaking this step down into a series of smaller, separate hurdles. The Third Step is just one more piece of the path of recovery from our addiction. Making the Third Step decision doesn't necessarily mean that we must suddenly, completely change everything about the way we live our lives. Fundamental changes in our lives happen gradually as we work on our recovery, and all such changes require our participation. We don't have to be afraid that this step will do something to us that we're not ready for or won't like.

It is significant that this step suggests we turn our will and our lives over to the *care of the God of our understanding*. These words are particularly important. By working the Third Step, we are allowing someone or something to *care for* us, not control us or conduct our lives for us. This step does not suggest that we become mindless robots with no ability to live our own lives, nor does it allow those of us who find such irresponsibility attractive to indulge such an urge. Instead, we are making a simple decision to change direction, to stop rebelling at the natural and logical flow of events in our lives, to stop wearing ourselves out trying to make everything happen as if we were in charge of the world. We are accepting that a Power greater than ourselves will do a better job of caring for our will and our lives than we have. We are furthering the spiritual process of recovery by beginning to explore what we understand the word "God" to mean to us as individuals.

In this step, each one of us will have to come to some conclusions about what we think "God" means. Our understanding doesn't have to be complex or complete. It doesn't have to be like anyone else's. We may discover that we're very sure what God *isn't* for us, but not what God *is*, and that's okay. The only thing that is essential is that we begin a search that will allow us to further our understanding as our recovery continues. Our concept of God will grow as we grow in our recovery. Working the Third Step will help us discover what works best for us.

Making a Decision

As we've already discussed, many of us may find ourselves unnerved by the thought of making a big decision. We may feel intimidated or overwhelmed. We may fear the results or the implied commitment. We may think it's a once-and-for-all action and fear that we won't do it right or have the opportunity to do it over again. However, the decision to turn our will and lives over to the care of the God of our understanding is one we *can* make over and over again, daily if need be. In fact, we're likely to find that we must make this decision regularly, or risk losing our recovery because of complacency.

It is essential that we involve our hearts and spirits in this decision. Though the word "decision" sounds like something that takes place mostly in the mind, we need to do the work necessary to go beyond an intellectual understanding and internalize this choice.

- Why is making a decision central to working this step?

- Can I make this decision just for today? Do I have any fears or reservations about it? What are they?

We need to realize that making a decision without following it up with action is meaningless. For example, we can decide one morning to go somewhere and then sit down and not leave our homes for the rest of that day. Doing so would render our earlier decision meaningless, no more significant than any random thought we may have.

- What action have I taken to follow through on my decision?

- What areas of my life are difficult for me to turn over?
  Why is it important that I turn them over anyway?

Self-will

Step Three is critical because we've acted on self-will for so long, abusing our right to make choices and decisions. So what exactly is self-will? Sometimes it's total withdrawal and isolation. We end up living a very lonely and self-absorbed existence. Sometimes self-will causes us to act to the exclusion of any considerations other than what we want. We ignore the needs and feelings of others. We barrel through, stampeding over anyone who questions our right to do whatever we want. We become tornadoes, whipping through the lives of family, friends, and even strangers, totally unconscious of the path of destruction we have left behind. If circumstances aren't to our liking, we try to change them by any means necessary to achieve our aims. We try to get our way at all costs. We are so busy aggressively pursuing our impulses that we completely lose touch with our conscience and with a Higher Power. To work this step, each one of us needs to identify the ways in which we have acted on self-will.

- How have I acted on self-will? What were my motives?

- How has acting on self-will affected my life?

- How has my self-will affected others?

Surrendering our self-will doesn't mean we can't pursue goals or try to make changes in our lives and the world. It doesn't mean we have to passively accept injustices to ourselves or to people for whom we're responsible. We need to differentiate between destructive self-will and constructive action.

- Will pursuing my goals harm anyone? How?

- In the pursuit of what I want, is it likely that I will end up doing something that adversely affects myself or others? Explain.

- Will I have to compromise any of my principles to achieve this goal?
  (For example: Will I have to be dishonest? Cruel? Disloyal?)

If we are new in the program and just beginning to work Step Three, we will probably end up wondering what God's will is for us, thinking that the step asks us to find this out. Actually, we don't formally focus our attention on seeking knowledge of our Higher Power's will for us until the Eleventh Step, but we do begin the process that will lead us to that point in Step Three.

God's will for us is something we will gradually come to know as we work the steps. At this point we can come to some very simple conclusions about our Higher Power's will for us that will serve us well for the time being. It is our Higher Power's will for us to stay clean. It is our Higher Power's will for us to do things that will help us stay clean, such as going to meetings and talking to our sponsor regularly.

- Describe the times when my will hasn't been enough. (For example, I couldn't stay clean on my own will.)

- What is the difference between my will and God's will?

At some point in our recovery, we may find that we have somehow shifted from trying to align our will with a Higher Power's to running on self-will. This happens so slowly and subtly that we hardly even notice. It seems as though we're especially vulnerable to self-will when things are going well. We cross the fine line that divides humble and honest pursuit of goals from subtle manipulation and forced results. We find ourselves going just a little too far in a discussion to convince someone that we are right. We find ourselves holding on to something just a little too long. We suddenly realize that we haven't contacted our sponsor in quite a while. We feel a quiet, almost subconscious discomfort that will alert us to this subtle shift away from recovery—if we listen.

- Have there been times in my recovery when I've found myself subtly taking back my will and my life? What alerted me? What have I done to recommit myself to the Third Step?

The God of Our Understanding

Before we delve deeply into the process of turning our will and our lives over to the care of the God of our understanding, we should work on overcoming any negative beliefs or unproductive preconceptions we may have about the word "God."

- Does the word "God," or even the concept itself, make me uncomfortable? What is the source of my discomfort?

- Have I ever believed that God caused horrible things to happen to me or was punishing me? What were those things?

Our Basic Text suggests that we choose an understanding of our Higher Power that is loving and caring and greater than ourselves. These simple guidelines can encompass as many understandings of God as there are NA members. They don't exclude anyone. If we understand the word "God" to mean the Power of the program, these guidelines fit. If we understand the word "God" to mean the spiritual principles of the program, these guidelines fit. If we understand the word "God" to mean a personal power or being with which we can communicate, these guidelines fit. It is essential that we begin exploring and developing our understanding. Our sponsor can help immeasurably in this process.

- What is my understanding of a Power greater than myself today?

- How is my Higher Power working in my life?

As important as it is to figure out what our Higher Power is to us, it is more important that we develop a relationship with whatever we understand that Power to be. We can do this in a variety of ways. First, we need to somehow communicate with our Higher Power. Some of us call this prayer, and some call it other things. This communication does not have to be formal, or even verbal.

Second, we need to be open to communication from our Higher Power. This may be done by paying attention to how we feel, our reactions, and what is going on inside and around us. Or we may have a personal routine that helps us connect with a Power greater than ourselves. It may be that our Higher Power speaks to us or helps us see the right thing to do through our fellow NA members.

Third, we need to allow ourselves to have feelings about the God of our understanding. We may get angry. We may feel love. We may feel frightened. We may feel grateful. It's okay to share the entire range of human emotion with our Higher Power. This allows us to feel closer to the Power upon which we rely and helps develop our trust in that Power.

- How do I communicate with my Higher Power?

- How does my Higher Power communicate with me?

- What feelings do I have about my Higher Power?

As many of us stay clean for some time, we work on developing an understanding of God for ourselves. Our growing understanding reflects our experiences. We mature into an understanding of God that gives us peace and serenity. We trust our Higher Power and are optimistic about life. We begin to feel that our lives are touched by something beyond our comprehension, and we are glad and grateful that this is so.

Then something happens that challenges everything we believe about our Higher Power or makes us doubt the existence of that Power altogether. It may be a death, or an injustice, or a loss. Whatever it is, it leaves us feeling as though we've been kicked in the stomach. We just can't understand it.

Times like these are when we need our Higher Power the most, though we probably find ourselves instinctively drawing away. Our understanding of a Higher Power is about to undergo a dramatic change. We need to keep reaching out to our Higher Power, asking for acceptance if not understanding. We need to ask for strength to go on. Eventually we will reestablish our relationship with our Higher Power, although probably on different terms.

- Am I struggling with changing beliefs about the nature of my Higher Power? Describe.

- Is my current concept of a Higher Power still working? How might it need to change?

As our understanding of a Higher Power grows and evolves, we'll find that we react differently to what goes on in our lives. We may find ourselves able to courageously face situations that used to strike fear in our hearts. We may deal with frustrations more gracefully. We may find ourselves able to pause and think about a situation before acting. We'll probably be calmer, less compulsive, and more able to see beyond the immediacy of the moment.

Turning It Over

The order in which we prepare to surrender our will and our lives to the care of the God of our understanding is significant. Many of us have found that we actually follow the order in the step: First, we turn over our will; then, gradually, we turn over our lives. It seems that it's easier for us to grasp the destructive nature of our self-will and see that it must be surrendered; consequently, it's usually the first to go. Harder for us to grasp is the need to turn over our lives and the process of that surrender.

For us to be comfortable with allowing our Higher Power to care for our lives, we will have to develop some trust. We may have no trouble turning over our addiction, but want to remain in control of the rest of our lives. We may trust our Higher Power to care for our work lives, but not our relationships. We may trust our Higher Power to care for our partners, but not our children. We may trust our Higher Power with our safety, but not our finances. Many of us have trouble letting go completely. We think we trust our Higher Power with certain areas of our lives, but immediately take back control the first time we get scared or things aren't going the way we think they should. It's necessary for us to examine our progress in turning it over.

- What does "to the care of" mean to me?

- What does it mean for me to turn my will and my life over to the care of the God of my understanding?

- How might my life be changed if I make the decision to turn it over to my Higher Power's care?

- How do I allow my Higher Power to work in my life?

- How does my Higher Power care for my will and my life?

- Have there been times when I have been unable to let go and trust God to care for the outcome of a particular situation? Describe.

- Have there been times when I *have* been able to let go and trust God for the outcome? Describe.

To turn our will and our lives over to the care of our Higher Power, we must take some kind of action. Many of us find that it works best for us to make some formal declaration on a regular basis. We may want to use the following quote from our Basic Text: "Take my will and my life. Guide me in my recovery. Show me how to live." This seems to capture the essence of Step Three for many of us. However, we can certainly feel free to find our own words, or to find a more informal way of taking action. Many of us believe that every day we abstain from using, or take suggestions from our sponsor, we are taking practical action on our decision to turn our will and lives over to the care of our Higher Power.

- How do I take action to turn it over? Are there any words I say regularly? What are they?

Spiritual Principles

In considering the spiritual principles intrinsic to Step Three, we will focus first on surrender and willingness. Then we will look at how hope translates into faith and trust. Finally, we will see how the principle of commitment is tied to the Third Step.

Practicing the principle of surrender is easy for us when everything is going along as we'd like—we think. Actually, when things are going smoothly, it's more likely that we are being lulled into a belief that we're in charge, which doesn't require much "surrender." Keeping the principle of surrender to the care of the God of our understanding alive in our spirits is essential, even when things are going well.

- What am I doing to reinforce my decision to allow my Higher Power to care for my will and my life?

- How does the Third Step allow me to build on the surrender I've developed in Steps One and Two?

We usually feel most willing immediately following a surrender. Willingness often comes in the wake of despair or a struggle for control. We can practice the principle of willingness, though, before it becomes necessary and possibly save ourselves some pain.

- In what ways have I demonstrated willingness in my recovery so far?

- Am I fighting anything in my recovery? What do I think would happen if I became willing to let recovery prevail in that area of my life?

There is a spiritual progression from hope to faith to trust in the Third Step. As we begin Step Three, we carry with us the sense of hope that was born in us as we worked the Second Step. Hope springs from the knowledge that our life is full of possibilities—there are no hard certainties yet, just the first whispers of anticipation that we just may be able to fulfill our heart's deepest desires. Lingering doubts fade as hope becomes faith. Faith propels us forward into action; we actually do the work that those we have faith in are telling us is necessary if we are to achieve what we want. In the Third Step, faith gives us the capacity to actually make a decision and carry that decision into action. Trust comes into play after faith has been applied. We have probably made significant progress toward fulfilling our goals; now we have evidence that we can influence the course of our lives through taking positive action.

- How have hope, faith, and trust become positive forces in my life?

- What further action can I take to apply the principles of hope, faith, and trust in my recovery?

- What evidence do I have that I can trust confidently in my recovery?

The principle of commitment is the culmination of the spiritual process of Step Three. Making the decision to "turn it over," over and over again, even when our decision doesn't seem to be having any positive effect, is what this step is all about. We can practice the spiritual principle of commitment by reaffirming our decision on a regular basis and by continuing to take action that gives our decision substance and meaning—for instance, working the rest of the steps.

- What have I done recently that demonstrates my commitment to recovery and to working a program? (For example: Have I taken a service position in NA? Have I agreed to sponsor another recovering addict? Have I continued to go to meetings no matter what I was feeling about them? Have I continued to work with my sponsor even after he or she told me an unpleasant truth or gave me some direction I didn't want to follow? Did I follow that direction?)

Moving on

As we get ready to go on to Step Four, we'll want to take a look at what we've gained by working Step Three. Writing about our understanding of each step as we prepare to move on helps us internalize the spiritual principles connected to it.

- Do I have any reservations about my decision to turn my will and my life over to God's care?

- Do I feel that I am now ready to turn it over?

- How does my surrender in the First Step help me in the Third Step?

- What action do I plan to take to follow through on my decision? How does working the remainder of the steps fit into this?

We wind up our work on Step Three with an increase in our level of freedom. If we've been thorough with this step, we're profoundly relieved to realize that the world will go along just fine without our intervention. The responsibility of running everything is a huge burden, and we're happy to lay it down. We may feel comforted that a loving God is caring for our will and our lives, letting us know in subtle ways that the path we're on is the right one. We've seen our old ideas for what they were, and we're willing to let go of them and allow change to happen in our lives. We may even find that we're willing to take some risks we never had the courage to take before, because we're secure in the knowledge of our Higher Power's care for us.

Some people pause before making major decisions and ground themselves in their own spirituality. We look to the source of our strength, invite our Higher Power to work in our lives, and move forward once we're sure we're on the right track. Now we need to take another step along the path of recovery, a step that makes our Third Step decision real. It's time to make a searching and fearless moral inventory of ourselves.

*"We made a searching
and fearless moral inventory
of ourselves."*

—Step Four

Most of us came to Narcotics Anonymous because we wanted to stop some-thing—using drugs. We probably didn't put much thought into what we were starting—a program of recovery—by coming to NA. But if we haven't taken a look at what we're getting out of this program, now might be a good time to pause and think about it.

First, we should ask ourselves what we want out of recovery. Most of us answer this question by saying that we just want to be comfortable, or happy, or serene. We just want to like ourselves. But how can we like ourselves when we don't even know who we are?

The Fourth Step gives us the means to begin finding out who we are, the information we'll need to begin to like ourselves and get those other things we expect from the program—comfort, happiness, serenity.

The Fourth Step heralds a new era in our recovery. Steps Four through Nine can be thought of as a process within a process. We will use the information we find in working the Fourth Step to work our Fifth, Sixth, Seventh, Eighth, and Ninth Steps. This process is meant to be done over and over again in recovery.

There is an analogy for this process that is particularly apt. We can think of ourselves as an onion. Each time we begin a Fourth Step, we are peeling away a layer of the onion and getting closer to the core. Each layer of the onion represents another layer of denial, the disease of addiction, our character defects, and the harm we've caused. The core represents the pure and healthy spirit that lies at the center of each one of us. It is our goal in recovery to have a spiritual awakening, and we get closer to that by beginning this process. Our spirits awaken a little more each time we go through it.

The Fourth Step is a method for learning about ourselves, and it is as much about finding our character assets as it is about identifying the exact nature of our wrongs. The inventory process is also an avenue to freedom. We have been prohibited from being free for so long—probably all our lives. Many of us have discovered, as we worked the Fourth Step, that our problems didn't begin the first time we took drugs, but long before, when the seeds of our addiction were actually planted. We may have felt iso-lated and different long before we took drugs. In fact, the way we felt and the forces that drove us are completely enmeshed with our addiction; it was our desire to change the way we felt and to subdue those forces that led us to take our first drug. Our inventory will lay bare the unresolved pain and conflicts in our past so that we are no longer at their mercy. We'll have a choice. We'll have achieved a measure of freedom.

This portion of the *Step Working Guides* actually has two distinct sections. The first helps us prepare to work the Fourth Step by guiding us through an exploration of our motives for working this step and what this step means to us. The second part is a guide for actually taking a searching and fearless moral inventory.

Motivation

Though our motivation for working the Fourth Step is not as important as actually working the Fourth Step, we may find it helpful to examine and dispel any reservations we have about this step, and think about some of the benefits we will get as a result of working this step.

- Do I have any reservations about working this step? What are they?

- What are some of the benefits that could come from making a searching and fearless moral inventory of myself?

- Why shouldn't I procrastinate about working this step?

- What are the benefits of not procrastinating?

Searching and Fearless

This is the phrase that has most puzzled many of us. We probably understand what "searching" means, but what about "fearless"? How can we get over all our fear? That might take years, we think; but we need to work on this inventory right away.

Taking a fearless inventory means going ahead despite our fear. It means having the courage to take this action no matter how we feel about it. It means having the courage to be honest, even when we're cringing inside and swearing that we'll take what we're writing to the grave. It means having the determination to be thorough, even when it seems that we've written enough. It means having the faith to trust this process and trust our Higher Power to give us whatever quality we need to walk through the process.

Let's face it: This step does involve a lot of work. But we can take heart from the fact that there's rarely a deadline on completing this step. We can do it in manageable sections, a little at a time, until we are done. The only thing that's important is that we work on it consistently.

There are times when our clean time can actually work against us: when we fail to acknowledge our fear of taking an inventory. Many of us who have worked the Fourth Step numerous times and know it's ultimately one of the most loving things we can do for ourselves may still find ourselves avoiding this task. We may think that since we know how good this process is, we shouldn't have any fear of it. But we need to give ourselves permission to be afraid, if that's what we feel.

We may also have fears that stem from our previous experiences with the Fourth Step. We know that an inventory means change in our lives. We know that if our inventories reveal destructive patterns, we can't continue to practice the same behaviors without a great deal of pain. Sometimes this means having to let go of something in our lives—some behavior we think we can't survive without; a relationship; or perhaps a resentment we've nursed so carefully that it's actually become, in a sick way, a source of reassurance and comfort. The fear of letting go of something we've come to depend on, no matter how much we've begun to suspect it isn't good for us, is an absolutely valid fear. We just can't let it stop us. We have to face it and act with courage.

We may also have to overcome a barrier that grows from an unwillingness to reveal more of our disease. Many of our members with clean time have shared that an inventory taken in later recovery revealed that their addiction had spread its tentacles so completely through their lives that virtually no area was left untouched. This realization is often initially met with feelings of dismay and perplexity. We wonder how we could still be so sick. Hasn't all this effort in recovery resulted in more than surface healing?

Of course it has. We just need some time to remember that. Our sponsor will be happy to remind us. After we've had time to accept what our inventories are revealing, we feel a sense of hope rising to replace the feelings of dismay. After all, an inventory always initiates a process of change and freedom. Why shouldn't it this time, too?

- Am I afraid of working this step? What is my fear?

- What does it mean to me to be searching and fearless?

- Am I working with my sponsor and talking to other addicts? What other action am I taking to reassure myself that I can handle whatever is revealed in this inventory?

A Moral Inventory

Many of us have a multitude of unpleasant associations connected to the word "moral." It may conjure up memories of an overly rigid code of behavior we were expected to adhere to. It may make us think of people we consider "moral," people we think of as better than ourselves. Hearing this word may also awaken our tendency toward rebellion against society's morals and our resentment of authorities who were never satisfied with our morality. Whether any of this is true for us, as individuals, is a matter to be determined by us, as individuals. If any of the preceding seems to fit, we can alleviate our discomfort with the word "moral" by thinking about it in a different way.

In Narcotics Anonymous, in this step, the word "moral" has nothing to do with specific codes of behavior, society's norms, or the judgment of some authority figure. A moral inventory is something we can use to discover our own individual morality, our own values and principles. We don't have to relate them in any way to the values and principles of others.

- Am I disturbed by the word "moral"? Why?

- Am I disturbed by thinking about society's expectations and afraid that I can't, won't, and will never be able to conform to them?

- What values and principles are important to me?

An Inventory of Ourselves

The Fourth Step asks us to take an inventory of ourselves, not of other people. Yet when we begin writing and looking at our resentments, fears, behavior, beliefs, and secrets, we will find that most of these are connected to another person, or sometimes to an organization or institution. It's important to understand that we are free to write whatever we need to about others, as long as it leads us to finding our part in the situation. In fact, most of us can't separate our part from their part at first. Our sponsor will help us with this.

Spiritual Principles

In the Fourth Step, we will call on all of the spiritual principles we began to practice in the first three steps. First of all, we have to be willing to work a Fourth Step. We'll need to be meticulously honest with ourselves, thinking about everything we write down and asking ourselves if it's true or not. We'll need to be courageous enough to face our fear and walk through it. Last, but not least, our faith and trust will carry us through when we're facing a difficult moment and feel like giving up.

- How is my decision to work Step Four a demonstration of courage? Trust? Faith? Honesty? Willingness?

The Inventory

Get a notebook or whatever means of recording your inventory you and your sponsor have agreed is acceptable. Get comfortable. Remove any distractions from the place where you plan to work on your inventory. Pray for the ability to be searching, fearless, and thorough. Don't forget to stay in touch with your sponsor throughout this process. Finally, feel free to go beyond what's asked in the following questions. Anything you think of is inventory material.

Resentments

We have resentments when we re-feel old feelings, when we are unable to let go, when we cannot forgive and forget something that has upset us. We list our resentments in the Fourth Step for a number of reasons. First, doing so will help us let go of old anger that is affecting our lives today. Second, exploring our resentments will help us identify the ways in which we set ourselves up to be disappointed in others, especially when our expectations were too high. Finally, making a list of our resentments will reveal patterns that kept us trapped in a cycle of anger, or self-pity, or both.

- What people do I resent? Explain the situations that led to the resentment.
- What institutions (school, government, religious, correctional, civic) do I resent?

Explain the situations that led to the resentment.

• What was my motivation, or what did I believe, that led me to act as I did in these situations?

• How has my dishonesty contributed to my resentments?

• How has my inability or unwillingness to experience certain feelings led me to develop resentments?

• How has my behavior contributed to my resentments?

• Am I afraid of looking at my part in the situations that caused my resentments? Why?

• How have my resentments affected my relationships with myself, with others, and with a Higher Power?

• What recurring themes do I notice in my resentments?

Feelings

We want to examine our feelings for much the same reason that we want to examine our resentments: It will help us discover our part in our own lives. In addition, most of us have forgotten how to feel by the time we get clean. Even if w e've been around awhile, we're still uncovering new information about the ways we've shut down our feelings.

• How do I identify my individual feelings?

• What feelings do I have the most trouble allowing myself to feel?

• Why have I tried to shut off my feelings?

• What means have I used to deny how I really felt?

• Who or what triggered a feeling? What was the feeling? What were the situations? What was my part in each situation?

• What was my motivation, or what did I believe, that led me to act as I did in these situations?

• What do I do with my feelings once I've identified them?

Guilt, Shame

There are actually two types of guilt or shame: one real, one imagined. The first grows directly out of our conscience—we feel guilty because we've done something that goes against our principles, or we harmed someone and feel shame over it. Imagined guilt results from any number of situations that are not our fault, situations we had no part in creating. We need to look at our guilt and shame so that we can separate these situations. We need to own what is truly ours and let go of what is not.

- Who or what do I feel guilty or ashamed about? Explain the situations that led to these feelings.

- Which of these situations have caused me to feel shame, though I had no part in creating them?

- In the situations I did have a part in, what was my motivation, or what did I believe, that led me to act as I did?

- How has my behavior contributed to my guilt and shame?

Fear

If we could look at the disease of addiction stripped of its primary symptoms—that is, apart from drug use or other compulsive behavior—and without its most obvious characteristics, we would find a swamp of self-centered fear. We're afraid of being hurt, or maybe of just having to feel too intensely, so we live a sort of half-life, going through the motions of living but never being fully alive. We're afraid of everything that might make us feel, so we isolate and withdraw. We're afraid that people won't like us, so we use drugs to be more comfortable with ourselves. We're afraid we'll get caught at something and have to pay a price, so we lie or cheat or hurt others to protect ourselves. We're afraid of being alone, so we use and exploit others to avoid feeling lonely or rejected or abandoned. We're afraid we won't have enough—of anything—so we selfishly pursue what we want, not caring about the harm we cause in the process. Sometimes, if we've gained things we care about in recovery, we're afraid we'll lose what we have, and so we begin compromising our principles to protect it. Self-centered, self-seeking fear— we need to uproot it so it no longer has the power to destroy.

- Who or what do I fear? Why?

- What have I done to cover my fear?

- How have I responded negatively or destructively to my fear?

- What do I most fear looking at and exposing about myself? What do I think will happen if I do?

- How have I cheated myself because of my fear?

Relationships

We need to write about our relationships in the Fourth Step—all of our relationships, not just the romantic ones—so that we can find out where our choices, beliefs, and behaviors have resulted in unhealthy or destructive relationships. We need to look at our relationships with relatives, spouses or partners, friends and former friends, co-workers and former co-workers, neighbors, people from school, people from clubs and civic organizations and the organizations themselves, authority figures such as the police, institutions, and anyone or anything else we can possibly think of. We should also examine our relationship with a Higher Power. We may be tempted to skip the relationships that didn't last long—a one-night sexual involvement, for instance, or perhaps an argument with a teacher whose class we then dropped. But these relationships are important, too. If we think of it or have feelings about it, it's inventory material.

- What conflicts in my personality make it difficult for me to maintain friendships and/or romantic relationships?

- How has my fear of being hurt affected my friendships and romantic relationships?

- How have I sacrificed platonic friendships in favor of romantic relationships?

- In what ways did I compulsively seek relationships?

- In my relationships with family, do I sometimes feel as though we're locked into repeating the same patterns over and over without any hope of change? What are those patterns? What is my part in perpetuating them?

- How have I avoided intimacy with my friends, partners or spouses, and family?

- Have I had problems making commitments? Describe.

- Have I ever destroyed a relationship because I believed I was going to get hurt anyway so I should get out before that could happen? Describe.

- To what degree do I consider the feelings of others in my relationships? Equal to my own? More important than my own? Of minor importance? Not at all?

- Have I felt like a victim in any of my relationships? (Note: This question is focused on uncovering how we set ourselves up to be victims or how too-high expectations contributed to our being disappointed in people, *not* on listing instances where we were actually abused.) Describe.

- What have my relationships with my neighbors been like? Do I notice any patterns appearing that carried through no matter where I lived?

- How do I feel about the people with and for whom I've worked? How have my thinking, beliefs, and behavior caused problems for me at work?

- How do I feel about the people I went to school with (both in childhood and currently)? Did I feel less than or better than the other students? Did I believe I had to compete for attention from the instructor? Did I respect authority figures or rebel against them?

- Have I ever joined any clubs or membership organizations? (Hint: NA is a membership organization.) How did I feel about the other people in the club or organization? Have I made friends in these organizations? Have I joined clubs with high expectations, only to quit in a short time? What were my expectations, and why weren't they fulfilled? What was my part in these situations?

- Have I ever been in a mental hospital or prison or otherwise been held against my will? What effect has that had on my personality? What were my interactions with the authorities like? Did I follow the rules? Did I ever break the rules and then resent the authorities when I got caught?

- Did early experiences with trust and intimacy hurt me and cause me to withdraw? Describe.

- Have I ever let a relationship go even when the potential existed to resolve conflicts and work through problems? Why?

- Did I become a different person depending on who I was around? Describe.

- Have I discovered things about my personality (perhaps in previous inventories) that I didn't like, and then found myself overcompensating for that behavior? (For instance, we may have uncovered a pattern of immature dependence on others and then overcompensated for this by becoming overly self-sufficient.) Describe.

- What defects are most often at play in my relationships (dishonesty, selfishness, control, manipulation, etc.)?

- How can I change my behavior so that I can begin having healthy relationships?

- Have I had any kind of a relationship with a Higher Power? How has this changed in my lifetime? What kind of a relationship do I have with my Higher Power now?

Sex

This is a very uncomfortable area for most of us. In fact, we may be tempted to stop here, thinking, "Okay, this has gone far enough! There's no way I'm cataloging my sexual behavior!" But we have to get over such unwillingness quickly. Thinking about the reason why we need to do this should help. As it says in *It Works: How and Why,* "We want to be at peace with our own sexuality." That's why we need to include our sexual beliefs and behaviors in our inventories. It's important to remind ourselves at this point that we are not taking our inventory to compare ourselves with what we think is "normal" for others, but only to identify our own values, principles, and morals.

- How was my sexual behavior based in selfishness?

- Have I confused sex with love? What were the results of acting on that confusion?

- How have I used sex to try to avoid loneliness or fill a spiritual void?

- In what ways did I compulsively seek or avoid sex?

- Have any of my sexual practices left me feeling ashamed and guilty? What were they? Why did I feel that way?

- Have any of my sexual practices hurt myself or others?

- Am I comfortable with my sexuality? If not, why not?

- Am I comfortable with others' sexuality? If not, why not?

- Is sex a prerequisite in all or most of my relationships?

- What does a healthy relationship mean to me?

Abuse

We must exercise extreme caution before beginning this section. In fact, we may need to postpone this section to a later time in our recovery. We should utilize all the resources at hand to make the decision about whether to begin this section now: our own sense of whether or not we're ready to withstand the pain this work will cause us, discussion with our sponsor, and prayer. Perhaps our sponsor will be able to help us through this, or we may need to seek additional help.

If we do decide to go ahead with this section, we should be aware that working on this area of our Fourth Step will probably be the most painful work we'll do in recovery. Recording the times when we were neglected or hurt by the people who were supposed to love and protect us is certain to cause some of the most painful feelings we will ever have to go through. It is important to do so when we're ready, however. As long as we keep the pain wrapped up inside us, a secret, it may cause us to act in ways we don't want, or it can contribute to a negative self-image or other destructive beliefs. Getting the truth out begins a process that can lead to the relief of our pain. We were not to blame.

- Have I ever been abused? By whom? What feelings did I or do I now have about it?

- Has being abused affected my relationships with others?
  How?

- If I have felt victimized for much of life because of being abused in childhood, what steps can I take to be restored to spiritual wholeness? Can my Higher Power help? How?

It is also possible that we have physically, mentally, or verbally abused others. Recounting these times is bound to cause us to feel a great deal of shame. We cannot afford to let that shame become despair. It is important that we face our behavior, accept responsibility for it, and work to change it. Writing about it here is the first step toward doing that. Working the rest of the steps will help us make amends for what we've done to others.

- Have I ever abused anyone? Who and how?

- What was I feeling and thinking right before I caused the harm?

- Did I blame my victim or make excuses for my behavior? Describe.

- Do I trust my Higher Power to work in my life and provide me with what I need so I don't have to harm anyone again? Am I willing to live with the painful feelings until they are changed through working the steps?

Assets

Most of the preceding questions have been directed at helping us identify the exact nature of our wrongs, information we'll need for the Fifth Step. It's also important that we take a look at things that we've done right or that have had a positive impact on ourselves and others. We want to do this for a couple of reasons. First, we want to have a complete picture of ourselves from working the Fourth Step, not a one-sided picture. Second, we want to know what character traits and behaviors we want more of in our lives.

- What qualities do I have that I like? That others like? That work well for me?

- How have I shown concern for myself and others?

- Which spiritual principles am I practicing in my life?
  How has doing so changed my life?

- How has my faith and trust in a Higher Power grown?

- What is my relationship with my sponsor based on?
  How do I see that positive experience translating into other relationships?

- What goals have I accomplished? Do I have other goals I am taking action to reach? What are they, and what action am I taking?

- What are my values? Which ones am I committed to living by, and how?

- How am I showing my gratitude for my recovery?

Secrets

Before we finish this Fourth Step, we should stop and reflect: Is there anything we've missed, either intentionally or not? Is there something we think is so bad that we just can't possibly include it in our inventory? If so, we should be reassured by the fact that a multitude of NA members have worked this step, and there has never yet been a situation in anyone's Fourth Step that was so unique that we had to create a new term to describe it. Keeping secrets is threatening to our recovery. As long as we are keeping a secret, we are actually building a reservation in our program.

- Are there any secrets that I haven't written about yet? What are they?

Another question we should ask ourselves now is, is there anything in this inventory that is either an exaggeration of what actually happened or something that's not true at all? Almost all of us came to NA and had trouble separating fact from fiction in our own lives. Most of us had accumulated "war stories" that were so embroidered that they may have contained only a fraction of truth. We made them up because we wanted to impress people. We didn't think we had anything to feel good about that was true, so we made up lies in an attempt to build ourselves up. But we don't have to do that anymore. We're building true self-worth in the process of working Step Four, not false self-worth based on some phony image. Now is the time to tell the truth about ourselves.

- Is there anything in this inventory that isn't true, or are there any stories I've told over and over again that aren't true?

Moving on

Finishing a Fourth Step is many things—may be a letdown, may be exhilarating, may be uncomfortable. However we feel otherwise, we should definitely feel good about what we've accomplished. The work we've done in this step will provide the foundation for the work we'll do in Steps Five through Nine. Now is the time to contact our sponsor and make arrangements to work Step Five.

*"We admitted to God,
to ourselves, and to another
human being the exact nature
of our wrongs."*

—Step Five

Our Basic Text tells us that "Step Five is not simply a reading of Step Four." Yet we know that reading our Fourth Step to another human being is certainly *part of* Step Five. So what's the rest, the part that's more than simply a reading.

It's the *admission* we make—to God, to ourselves, and to another human being—that brings about the spiritual growth connected with this step. We've had some experience with making admissions already. We've admitted we have a disease; we've admitted we need help; we've admitted there's a Power that could help us. Drawing on our experience with these admissions will help us in Step Five.

Many of us finished our Fourth Step with a sense of relief, thinking that the really hard part was over, only to realize that we still had the Fifth Step to do. That's when the fear set in.

Some of us were afraid that our sponsor would reject or judge us. Others hesitated because we didn't want to bother our sponsor with so much. We weren't sure we trusted our sponsor to keep our secrets.

We may have been concerned about what the inventory might reveal. There might be something hidden from us that our sponsor would spot immediately—and it probably wouldn't be anything good. Some of us were afraid of having to re-feel old feelings, and wondered if there was really any benefit to stirring up the past. Some of us felt that as long as we hadn't actually spoken our inventories out loud, the contents wouldn't be quite real.

If we consider all our feelings about the Fifth Step, we may find that we are also motivated to continue this process by a desire for more recovery. We think about the people we know who have worked this step. We're struck by their genuineness and by their ability to connect with others. They aren't always talking about themselves. They're asking about others, and they're truly interested in knowing the answer. And if we ask them how they learned so much about relationships with others, they'll probably tell us that they began learning when they worked Step Five.

Many of us, having worked the Fourth and Fifth Steps before, knew that this process always resulted in change—in other words, we'd have to stop behaving the same old way! We may not have been entirely sure we wanted that. On the other hand, many of us knew we had to change, but were afraid we couldn't.

Two things we need to begin working Step Five are courage and a sense of trust in the process of recovery. If we have both these things, we'll be able to work through more specific fears and go through with the admissions we need to make in this step.

Facing Fears

Any of the fears we've talked about here might be ours, or we might have other fears that plague us. It's essential that we know what our fears are and move forward in spite of them so that we're able to continue with our recovery.

45

• What reservations do I have about working the Fifth Step?

• Do I have any fears at this point? What are they?

No matter what our fears stem from, most of our members have done pretty much the same things to deal with them: We pray for courage and willingness, read the section from It Works: How and Why on the Fifth Step, and seek reassurance from other members. Many of us have had the experience of going to step study meetings and finding that, coincidentally, the topic always seems to be Step Four or Five. If we make the effort to share what we're going through, we're sure to get the support we need from other members. Calling upon the spiritual resources we have developed through working the previous steps will allow us to proceed with our Fifth Step.

• What am I doing to work through my fears about doing a Fifth Step?

• How has working the first four steps prepared me to work the Fifth Step?

Admitted to God

The chapter on Step Five in It Works: How and Why answers the question about why we must admit the exact nature of our wrongs to God in addition to admitting them to ourselves and another human being. In NA, we experience a way of life where the spiritual meets the everyday, where the ordinary meets the extraordinary. When we admit the exact nature of our wrongs to the God of our understanding, our admission becomes more meaningful.

How we make our admission to the God of our understanding depends on the specifics of our understanding. Some make a formal admission to God apart from the admissions we make to ourselves and another human being. Others acknowledge or invite the presence of a Higher Power in some way before going over the inventory with their sponsor. Those of us whose Higher Power is the spiritual principles of recovery or the power of the NA Fellowship may have to explore different methods of working this portion of the Fifth Step. Our sponsor can help with this process. Whatever we do is okay as long as we are aware that we are also making our admission to a Higher Power.

• How will I include the God of my understanding in my Fifth Step?

• How is my Third Step decision reaffirmed by working the Fifth Step?

To Ourselves

When we were using, most of us probably had people telling us we had a drug problem and should get some help. Their comments didn't really matter to us. Or even if they did matter, it wasn't enough to stop us from using. Not until we admitted our addiction to ourselves and surrendered to the NA program were we able to stop using. It's just the same with the admission we make in the Fifth Step. We can have everyone from our spouse to our employer to our sponsor telling us what we're doing that's working against us, but until we admit to our own innermost selves the exact nature of our wrongs, we're not likely to have the willingness or the ability to choose another way.

- Can I acknowledge and accept the exact nature of my wrongs?
- How will making this admission change the direction of my life?

And to another Human Being

As addicts, one of the biggest problems we have is telling the difference between our responsibility and the responsibilities of others. We blame ourselves for catastrophes over which we have no control. Conversely, we're often in complete denial about how we have hurt ourselves and others. We overdramatize minor troubles, and we shrug off major problems we really should be taking a look at. If we're not sure what the exact nature of our wrongs is when we begin our Fifth Step, we'll know by the time we finish— because of making our admissions to another human being. What we can't see, our listener can, and he or she will help us sort out what we need to accept as our responsibility and what we don't.

Most of us asked someone to be our sponsor before we began formally working the steps, and have been developing a relationship with that person ever since. For most of us, our sponsor will be the "another human being" we choose to hear our Fifth Step. He or she will help us separate the things that were not our responsibility from the things that were. The relationship we have been building with our sponsor will give us the trust we need to have in him or her. The therapeutic value of one addict helping another is often powerfully demonstrated when our sponsor shares details from his or her own inventory as we share ours. This goes a long way toward reassuring us that we are not unique.

The trust we must have in the person who is to hear our Fifth Step goes beyond simply being assured that he or she will keep our confidences. We need to trust that our listener can respond appropriately to what we are sharing. One of the primary reasons that so many of us find ourselves choosing our sponsor as the person who will listen to our Fifth Step is because he or she understands what we're doing and therefore knows just what kind of support we need during this process. Also, if our sponsor is our listener, it will help promote continuity when we work the following steps. Still, if for any reason we choose someone else to hear our Fifth Step admission, his or her "qualifications" are the same ones we would look for in our sponsor: an ability to be supportive without minimizing our responsibility, someone who can provide a steadying influence if we begin to feel overwhelmed during our Fifth Step—in short, someone with compassion, integrity, and insight.

- What qualities does my listener have that are attractive to me?
- How will his or her possession of these qualities help me make my admissions more effectively?

For most of us, developing an honest relationship is something new. We're very good at running away from relationships the first time someone tells us a painful truth. We're also good at having polite, distant interactions with no real depth. The Fifth Step helps us to develop honest relationships. We tell the truth about who we are—then, the hard part: We listen to the response. Most of us have been terrified of having a relationship like this. The Fifth Step gives us a unique opportunity to try such a relationship in a safe context. We can be pretty much assured that we won't be judged.

• Am I willing to trust the person who is to hear my Fifth Step?

• What do I expect from that person?

• How will working the Fifth Step help me begin to develop new ways of having relationships?

The Exact Nature of Our Wrongs

Another way to ensure that our Fifth Step is "not simply a reading of Step Four" is to focus on what we are supposed to be admitting: the *exact nature* of our wrongs. There is a diversity of experience in our fellowship about what, precisely, is "the exact nature of our wrongs." Most of us agree that, in working Step Five, we should be focusing our attention on what's behind the patterns of our addiction and the reasons we acted out in the ways we did. Identifying the exact nature of our wrongs is often something that happens while we're sharing our inventory. Sometimes the repetition of the same type of situation will reveal the exact nature of that situation. Why do we, for example, keep choosing to involve ourselves with people who don't have our best interests at heart? Why do we keep approaching every relationship we have as though our very lives depended on having the upper hand? Why do we feel threatened by new experiences, and so keep avoiding them? Finding the common thread in our own patterns will lead us right to the exact nature of our wrongs.

At some point in this process, we will probably begin calling certain patterns of behavior our "character defects." Though it won't be until the Sixth Step that we begin an in-depth examination of how each one of our defects plays a role in keeping us sick, it certainly won't hurt to allow this knowledge to begin forming in us now.

• How does the exact nature of my wrongs differ from my actions?

• Why do I need to admit the *exact nature* of my wrongs, and not just the wrongs themselves?

Spiritual Principles

In the Fifth Step, we will focus on trust, courage, self-honesty, and commitment. Practicing the spiritual principle of trust is essential if we are to get through the Fifth Step. As mentioned above, we will probably have some experience with our sponsor that allows us to trust him or her enough to go ahead with this step; but what about the more profound issues that arise when we wonder if working this step will really do any good? We have to trust a process as well as another person. The connection between the Fifth Step and our spiritual development isn't always clear to us. This doesn't mean that the connection is any less real, but it may make it harder for us to trust the process.

- Do I believe that working the Fifth Step will somehow make my life better? How?

Courage is one principle we'll have to practice just to get started on this step. We'll probably need to continue drawing on our courage periodically throughout our work on this step. When we replace the phone on its hook just as we are about to call our sponsor for an appointment to make our admissions, we're feeling fear and we need to practice courage. When we're sharing our inventory and we see a paragraph that we just can't tell anyone about, we need to face that moment of fear with courage and go ahead with sharing *all* of our inventory. When we've just shared something excruciatingly pain-ful, and our feelings of vulnerability are so overwhelming that we want to shut down before we hear what our sponsor has to say, we're at a defining moment in our recovery and we need to choose the courageous path. Doing so will influence the future course of our lives. Each time we feel fear, we remind ourselves that giving in to it has rarely had anything but negative consequences in our lives, and doing so this time won't be any different. Such a reminder should be sufficient to motivate us to gather our courage.

- What are some of the ways in which I can find the courage I need to work this step?
- How does practicing the principle of courage in working this step affect my whole recovery?
- Have I set a time and place for my Fifth Step? When and where?

Practicing the principle of self-honesty is essential when we admit to ourselves the exact nature of our wrongs. Just as we mustn't disassociate ourselves from our emo-tions simply because we're afraid of our listener's response, so we can't afford to shut down our own reactions. We must allow ourselves to experience the natural and human reaction to the subject under discussion: our lives as addicts. Our lives have been sad. We've missed out on a lot because of our addiction. We've hurt people we loved be-cause of our addiction. These realizations are painful. However, if we pay close atten-tion, we'll probably recognize another feeling that's beginning to form in the wake of the pain: hope.

We've finally stopped using over our feelings, running away from our feelings, and shutting down because of our feelings; now, for the first time, we have a chance to walk through our feelings, even the painful ones, with courage. Doing so will, in the long run, make us feel better about ourselves. This is one of the paradoxes that we often find in recovery. What begins in pain ends in joy and serenity.

- How have I avoided self-honesty in the past? What am I doing to practice it now?

- How is a more realistic view of myself connected to humility?

- How does practicing the principle of self-honesty help me accept myself?

The principle of commitment is demonstrated by the action we take in this step. Many of us have made so-called "commitments" in our lives, commitments which we had no intention of sticking to in tough times; our "commitments" were made solely for the sake of convenience. With each step we've taken in the program of NA, we've deepened our real, practical commitment to the program. Getting a sponsor, working the steps, finding a home group and going to its meetings—each one of these actions demonstrates that we're committed to our recovery in a practical, meaningful way.

- How does sharing my inventory with my sponsor further my commitment to the NA program?

Moving on

One of the many benefits we get from working Step Five is a sense of self-acceptance. We clearly recognize who we are today, and accept ourselves without reservation. Just because we're lacking in certain areas doesn't mean we're worthless. We begin to see that we have both assets and defects. We're capable of great good—and of inflicting great harm. There are aspects of our personalities that make us very special. Our experiences, even the negative ones, have often contributed to the development of the very best parts of us. For the first time, we're able to acknowledge that we're okay just as we are, right at this moment. But accepting ourselves as we are today doesn't mean we can relax and stop striving for improvement. True self-acceptance includes accepting what we're lacking. It wouldn't be self-acceptance if we believed we had no further growing to do—it would be denial. So we acknowledge what we're lacking, and we make a commitment to work on it. If we want to be more compassionate, we work on it by practicing the principle of compassion. If we want to be better educated, we take the time to learn. If we want to have more friends, we take the time to develop our relationships.

- How has working Step Five increased my humility and self-acceptance?

As we finish Step Five, we may feel a sense of relief; we've unburdened ourselves by sharing what we previously had put a lot of energy into hiding or suppressing. It is true that our "defects... die in the light of exposure." Exposure to the light brings a sense of freedom that we feel no matter what the outer circumstances of our lives may be like.

All of our relationships begin to change as a result of working this step. We especially need to acknowledge how much our relationships with ourselves, with a Higher Power, and with other people have changed:

- How has my relationship with a Higher Power changed as a result of working the Fifth Step?

- How has my relationship with my sponsor changed as a result of working the Fifth Step?

- How has my view of myself changed as a result of working this step?

- To what extent have I developed love and compassion for myself and others?

Along with a sense of relief, our weariness with our character defects has probably reached a peak. This will translate easily into a state of being entirely ready—just what we need to begin Step Six!

"We were entirely ready to have God remove all these defects of character."

—Step Six

We begin working Step Six full of the hope we have developed in the first five steps. If we have been thorough, we have also developed some humility. In Step Six, "humility" means that we're able to see ourselves more clearly. We've seen the exact nature of our wrongs. We've seen how we've harmed ourselves and others by acting on our defects of character. We've seen the patterns of our behavior, and we've come to understand how we are likely to act on the same defects over and over. Now we have to become entirely ready to have our defects of character removed.

Becoming entirely ready won't happen in an instant. It's a long process, often taking place over the course of a whole lifetime. Immediately following an inventory, we may feel very ready indeed to have our defects removed. If we've been around awhile and are generally pretty well aware of what our defects are, and we still act on one of them, we'll naturally find that our willingness level rises. Awareness alone will never be enough to ensure our readiness, but it's the necessary first step on the path to readiness. The inventory process itself has raised our awareness about our character defects; working the Sixth Step will do so even more. To be entirely ready is to reach a spiritual state where we are not just aware of our defects; not just tired of them; not just confident that the God of our understanding will remove what should go—but all these things.

In order to become entirely ready, we'll need to address our fears about the Sixth Step. We'll also need to take a look at how our defects will be removed. The Sixth Step says that only a Higher Power can remove them, but what does that mean in practical terms? What is our responsibility in the Sixth Step? These questions, when reviewed with a sponsor, will help give us direction in working this step.

Entirely Ready for *What*?

If we're new in NA and this is our first experience with the Sixth Step, many of our character defects will be so blatant that our immediate reaction will likely be one of overwhelming willingness to get rid of them. We're seeing them for the first time, in all their glory, so to speak, and we want them gone—today!

Once we've gotten past our initial reaction, we'll find that we probably have at least some measure of fear or uncertainty about changing. The unknown is terrifying for almost everyone. We've had the defects we're about to let go of for a long time, probably most of our lives.

We probably have some fears about what our lives will be like without these defects. Some of them may seem more like vital survival skills than defects of character. We wonder if the removal of our defects will inhibit our ability to earn a living. We may find that the idea of being a "respectable citizen" is repulsive to us. Many of us are strongly attached to an image—we're cool, we're trendy, we're outside the bounds of polite society, and we like it that way. We may be afraid that by working the Sixth Step we'll be changed into dull conformists. Some of us may think that we're nothing but defects, and wonder what will be left of us if our defects are removed. Our fears are probably vague and unformed. If we pursue them to their logical conclusion, we're sure to find that they are unfounded. In other words, if we say them out loud, we can see them for what they are.

- Are there parts of me I like, but which might be "defects"? Am I afraid I'll turn into someone I don't like if those parts of my character are removed?
- What do I think will be removed?

If we've had some previous experience with the Sixth Step, our character defects are nothing new. In fact, we may be feeling dismayed right now that we still have a certain defect, or we may be upset because we're looking at the same old defect in a new manifestation.

For instance, we're still insecure. We may no longer run around indulging in a series of transparent attempts to convince others that we're big shots, but we still have the defect. The way we've been acting on it lately is far more subtle and far more insidious. We may have been unconsciously sabotaging the efforts of others so that we can look better by comparison, or trampling on someone else's desires because they don't directly serve our own needs. What's especially painful about realizations such as this in later recovery is that we've tended to think of ourselves in a better light. We're deeply ashamed of harming others. We may feel a dull fear that we're incapable of change, that one character defect or another is here to stay. We can draw some measure of comfort from the fact that we're now aware of what we've been doing and are willing to work on it. We need to maintain a sense of hope and trust that the process of recovery works even on the most firmly entrenched defects.

- Do I still believe in the process of recovery? Do I believe I can change? How have I changed so far? What defects do I no longer have to act on?
- Do I have any defects that I think cannot be removed? What are they? Why do I think they cannot be removed?

...to Have God Remove...

Yes, the Sixth Step specifies that only a Power greater than ourselves can remove our defects of character. However, the extent to which most of us grasp what that actually means is directly influenced by how much experience we have with the up-and-down, on-again-off-again struggle and surrender associated with Step Six.

The first thing most of us do about our character defects is decide not to have them. Unfortunately, this is futile—about as effective as attempting to control our using. We may have some apparent success for a time, but our defects will eventually resurface. The problem is that our defects are part of us. We will always be subject to reverting to our worst character defects in stressful situations.

What we need to do in the Sixth Step is much like what we had to do in the first two steps. We have to admit that we have been defeated by an internal force that has brought nothing but pain and degradation to our lives; then, we have to admit we need help in dealing with that force. We must completely accept the fact that we cannot remove our own shortcomings, and we must prepare ourselves to ask in the Seventh Step for God to remove them for us.

- How am I trying to remove or control my own character defects? What have my attempts resulted in?

- What is the difference between being entirely ready to have God remove my defects of character and suppressing them myself?

- How am I increasing my trust in the God of my understanding by working this step?

- How does my surrender deepen in this step?

- What action can I take that shows that I am entirely ready?

Our Defects of Character

Even after all the work we've done in the Fourth and Fifth Steps, we're still not entirely clear at this point about the nature of our defects of character. We're probably wondering where, precisely, our character *defects* end and our *character* begins within the complex structure of our personality. Why do we do the things we do? Is it someone's fault? When did we first feel this way? Why? How? Where? If we're not careful, we can become so self-obsessed that we lose sight of why we're working a Sixth Step. We need to focus our efforts. Our goal is to raise our awareness of our character defects so that we can become entirely ready to have them removed, not to analyze their origin or indulge in a bout of self-absorption.

Our character defects are indicators of our basic nature. We are likely to find that we have the same basic nature as anyone else. We have needs, and we try to get them met. For instance, we need love. How we go about getting love is where our defects come into play. If we lie, cheat, or harm others and degrade ourselves to get love, we are acting on defects. As defined in *It Works: How and Why*, our defects are basic human traits that have been distorted by our self-centeredness. With our sponsor's help, we need to list each defect we have, describe the ways in which we act on it, look at how it affects our lives, and, very importantly, find out what we're feeling when we practice it. Imagining what our life would be like without each defect will help us see that we can live without it. Some of us take practical action by finding out what the opposite spiritual principle would be for each character defect.

- List each defect, and give a brief definition of it.

- In what ways do I act on this defect?

- When I act on this defect, what effect does it have on myself and others?

- What feelings do I associate with this defect? Am I trying to suppress certain feelings by acting on certain defects?

- What would my life be like without this behavior? Which spiritual principle can I apply instead?

Spiritual Principles

In the Sixth Step, we will focus on commitment and perseverance, willingness, faith and trust, and self-acceptance. At this point in our Sixth Step work, we should be acutely aware of our shortcomings. In fact, we're probably so aware of them that, in the course of our daily lives, we can see them coming and even stop ourselves from acting on them much of the time. At times, our awareness may fade, and we may no longer be as vigilant in watching our behavior. It takes an incredible amount of energy to monitor ourselves every second and curb every impulse to act out. We'll relax into everyday life until, all of a sudden, we'll be left feeling sick and ashamed and wondering how, after all the work we've done, we could have possibly done *that* again.

However, we do not give up. Instead, we make a commitment to our recovery. We maintain our newly emerging principles despite our setback. We keep taking steps forward even though we've taken one or more backward. We're looking for gradual improvement, not instant faultlessness.

- How am I demonstrating my commitment to recovery today?

- By working the first five steps, I have persevered in my recovery. Why is this quality so vital to the Sixth Step?

Applying the spiritual principle of willingness means, very simply, that we are willing to act differently. It does not necessarily mean that we will act differently or even that we're capable of doing so. We can perhaps best illustrate this attitude by an example. Suppose we've been dishonest—with our families, with our employers, with our friends— in many ways, ranging from the minor to the severe. While it may seem better to become willing in "layers," focusing our willingness on the worst or most destructive forms of dishonesty first, this step says that we were *entirely* ready to have *all* our defects removed. That means being willing never to be dishonest again, even in a minor way. This may seem like more than we can expect of ourselves, but we only have to do it for today.

It's hard to have this kind of willingness, especially when the apparent consequences for mild dishonesty aren't so severe. We may be aware that we're not being entirely honest, but we think we're not hurting anyone and we're getting away with it, so why be concerned about it? But it's this kind of thinking that has perhaps the most severe spiritual consequences. It may turn out that no one is obviously harmed by our dishonesty, and that no one ever finds out, but the dishonesty reverberates in our spirits from then on. Even if we're not consciously aware of it, even if we sleep just fine at night, the result of acting on a defect when we have the ability not to is an impairment of our spiritual growth. If we continue being unwilling, we'll eventually paralyze our spiritual growth.

- Am I willing to have all my defects of character removed at this time? If not, why not?

- What have I done to show my willingness today?

The amount of willingness we have to develop in this step requires a corresponding amount of faith and trust. We have to believe that a Higher Power is going to work in our lives to the exact degree that's necessary. Continuing with the example of dishonesty, we have to trust that our Higher Power isn't going to remove the defect of dishonesty from our lives to such a degree that we become brutally honest, incapable of remaining silent even when speaking the truth would hurt someone. As long as we get out of the way so that God can work in our lives, we'll experience the exact degree of spiritual growth we need.

- To what degree is my fear of what I will become still present? Has it diminished since I began working this step?

- How am I increasing my trust in the God of my understanding by working this step?

With words like "entirely" and "all" playing such a prominent role in this step, it's easy to become overly self-critical and perfectionistic. We need to remember that even though our willingness must be complete, we're not going to become perfect—not today, not ever. When we act out on a defect against our will, we need to practice the principle of self-acceptance. We need to accept that while we're still capable of acting out, we're also still willing to change; with that acknowledgment, we renew our commitment to be changed. We've grown exactly as much as we were supposed to for today, and if we were perfect, we would have no further need to grow.

- Do I accept myself today? What do I like about myself? What has changed since I've been working the steps?

Moving on

We may have had fleeting glimpses in the past of what we could become—maybe during childhood, maybe during our active addiction. We probably thought either that life didn't put us in a place where we could become what we dreamed of, or that we were just innately incapable of rising to a higher place. We may once have dreamed of money, or status, or position. In the spiritual program of Narcotics Anonymous, we're more concerned with spiritual growth. We want to think about qualities we wish we had, or about other people we know in recovery who have qualities we wish to emulate.

As we work this step, we begin developing a vision of the person we'd like to become. If we have been selfish, we probably have a vision of becoming selfless, maybe by helping another addict find recovery or by some other act of selfless giving. If we've been lazy, we may see ourselves becoming productive and reaping the rewards of our efforts. If we've been dishonest, we may have a dream of the freedom that can be ours when we no longer have to spend so much time worrying about being found out. We want to get from this step a vision of ourselves and a sense of hope that we can attain that vision.

- What do I see myself doing with the qualities I wish to attain?
  What will I do with my career? What will I do in my spare time?
  What kind of parent, child, partner, or friend will I be? Be specific.

This vision can be our inspiration. Recalling it during the times when we feel despair, or when it seems to be taking a long time to reach our goals, will sustain us and help us renew our willingness. Our vision is our springboard into Step Seven, where we'll ask the God of our understanding to remove our shortcomings.

"We humbly asked Him to remove our shortcomings."

—Step Seven

Though each of the Twelve Steps is a separate process unto itself, they all blend together to some degree as their parts interact with one another aspects of Step One fusing into Step Two, components of Step Four meshing into the following steps. Perhaps the finest line between two steps is the one between Steps Six and Seven. At first glance, Step Seven may seem almost an afterthought to Step Six. We spent a great deal of time and effort raising our awareness of our character defects in Step Six and getting to the point where we were entirely ready to have them removed; now all we need to do is ask, right?

Not exactly. There's much more to this step than just filing a request with our Higher Power and waiting for a response. There's spiritual preparation. There's the need to develop an understanding about what "humbly" means in this context. There's the need to find a way of asking that fits into our individual spiritual paths. And there's the need to practice spiritual principles in the place of character defects.

Preparing to Work Step Seven

We've already done much of the spiritual preparation we'll need to begin Step Seven. It's important that we draw the connection between the work we've done and the results that work has produced.

The previous steps have all served to sow the seeds of humility in our spirits. In this step, those seeds take root and grow. Many of us have difficulty with the concept of humility, and while we began addressing this issue in Step Six, it merits attention in Step Seven, too. We need to understand what humility is for us and how its presence is revealed in our lives.

We should not confuse humility with humiliation. When we are humiliated, we are ashamed; we feel worthless. Humility is almost the complete opposite of this feeling. Through working the steps, we've been stripping away layers of denial, ego, and self-centeredness. We have also been building a more positive self-image and practicing spiritual principles. Before, we couldn't see our strengths because the good, healthy part of us was hidden behind our disease. Now we can. That is humility. Some examples of how humility is often revealed may help us understand this concept.

We started out in recovery with fixed ideas. Since we've been in recovery, everything we believed in the past has been challenged. We've been barraged with new ideas. For instance, if we believed we were in control, just the fact that we've wound up in NA admitting our powerlessness was probably enough to change our outlook. Because of our addiction, we failed to learn the lessons that life itself would have taught us about how much control one individual has. Through our abstinence and the working of the first six steps, we have learned a great deal about how to live.

Many of us came to NA with a certain "street" mentality. The only way we knew to get what we wanted was by approaching it indirectly and manipulating people. We didn't realize that we could just be forthright and have the same chance, if not better, of fulfilling our needs. We spent years learning to blank our facial expressions, hide our compassion, and harden ourselves. By the time we arrived in NA, we were very good at it—so good, in fact, that novice addicts were probably looking to our example the same way we looked to older addicts when we first started using. We learned to suppress all humanity and became, in many cases, completely inhuman.

Removing ourselves from the arena in which such games are played exposed us to new ideas. We learned that it was okay to have feelings and to show them. We found out that the rules of the street only made sense on the street; in the real world, they were crazy and often dangerous. We became softer, more vulnerable. We no longer mistook kindness for weakness.

Changing these attitudes has a dramatic effect. Oftentimes, it even changes our physical appearance. Knotted brows and jaws relax into smiles. Tears flow freely out, uncovering our drowning spirit.

Many of us arrived in NA convinced that we were victims of bad luck, unfavorable circumstances, and conspiracies to thwart our good intentions. We believed we were good people, but profoundly misunderstood. We justified any harm we caused as self-defense, if we were capable of realizing that we caused harm at all. Feelings of self-pity went hand-in-hand with that attitude. We reveled in our suffering, and we secretly knew that the payoff for our pain was never, ever having to look at our part in anything.

But the first six steps get us to begin to do just that—we look at our part in things. Once we thought that certain situations happened *to* us; now we see how those situations were really created *by* us. We become aware of all the opportunities we've wasted. We stop blaming other people for our lot in life. We begin to see that where we've ended up has been determined mostly by the choices we've made.

Humility is a sense of our own humanness. If this is our first experience with the Seventh Step, this may be the point when we first feel a sense of compassion for ourselves. It's deeply moving to realize for the first time that we're truly just human and trying our best. We make decisions, both good and bad, and hope things turn out okay. With this knowledge about who we are, we also realize that just as we're doing our best, so are other people. We feel a real connection with others, knowing that we're all subject to the same insecurities and failings and that we all have dreams for the future.

Now we need to acknowledge our own humility and explore how it makes itself known in our everyday lives.

- Which of my attitudes have changed since I've been in recovery? Where has the overblown been deflated, and where has the healthy part of me been uncovered?

- How does humility affect my recovery?

- How does being aware of my own humility help when working this step?

Our work in the previous steps has helped us build a relationship with a God of our own understanding. That work will pay off in a big way as we proceed with Step Seven. In Step Two, we first began to think about a Higher Power that could help us find recovery from our addiction. From there, we went on to make our Third Step decision to trust our Higher Power with the care of our will and lives. We called upon that Power many times to get us through Step Four, and then in the Fifth Step shared with that Power the most intimate details of our lives. In Step Six, we discovered that the God of our understanding could do more for us than just keep us clean.

- How has my understanding of a Higher Power grown in the previous steps? How has my relationship with that Power developed?

- How has my work on the previous steps made me ready to work the Seventh Step?

Asking to Have Our Shortcomings Removed

So how do we ask the God of our understanding to remove our shortcomings? The answer is likely to depend a great deal on what kind of understanding we have of God. There are many, many different ways to understand God, so many that we couldn't possibly provide examples in this guide of how each person's individual spiritual path would influence his or her Seventh Step work. Suffice it to say that our step work should reflect our own spiritual paths.

As individuals, we might pick a particular personal routine or ritual as our way of asking our Higher Power to remove our shortcomings. For the purposes of this guide, we will call that "prayer." The word "prayer" is widely accepted in our fellowship as a description of the way we communicate with our Higher Power. The tone of asking is captured in the word "humbly." Coming from the place in ourselves that is most honest, the place that's closest to our spiritual center, we ask to have our shortcomings removed.

- How will I ask the God of my understanding to remove my shortcomings?

- Can other recovering addicts help me figure out how I'm going to ask? Have I asked them to share their experience, strength, and hope with me? Have I asked my sponsor for guidance?

As with any other aspect of our program, we're not going to ask just once to have our shortcomings removed. We'll ask again and again throughout our lifetimes. The way we ask is certain to change as our understanding of God changes. Nothing we do at this point locks us into one way of working the Seventh Step forever.

Getting Out of the Way

Most of us realize that we probably need to do something more in this step than just pray for our shortcomings to be removed. We need to take some action that will invite the God of our understanding to work in our lives. We can't ask God to remove a short-coming, then hang on to it with all our might. The more distance we keep between ourselves and our Higher Power, the less we will feel that Power's presence. We have to maintain the awareness of ourselves that we gained in the Sixth Step, and add to it an awareness of God working in our lives.

- How does the spiritual principle of surrender apply to getting out of the way so a Higher Power can work in our lives?

- What might be the benefits of allowing a Higher Power to work in my life?

- How do I feel, knowing that a Higher Power is caring for me and working in my life?

Spiritual Principles

In the Seventh Step, we will focus on surrender, trust and faith, patience, and humility. In the Seventh Step, we take our surrender to a deeper level. What began in Step One with an acknowledgment of our addiction now includes an acknowledgment of the short-comings that go along with our addiction. We also take our Second Step surrender to a deeper level. We come to believe that our Higher Power can do more than help us stay clean. We look to that Power to relieve us of our shortcomings as well. As time goes by, we place more and more of our trust in a Higher Power and in the process of recovery.

- Have I accepted my powerlessness over my shortcomings as well as my addiction? Expand on this.

- How has my surrender deepened?

The spiritual principles of trust and faith are central to the Seventh Step. We must be sure enough of our Higher Power to trust that Power with our shortcomings. We have to believe our Higher Power is going to do something with them, or how can we ask with any faith that they be removed? We must avoid any tendency to keep score of how we think God's doing in removing our defects. It's not too hard to see where this kind of thinking can lead if we find we still have certain character defects after some arbitrary amount of time has passed. Instead, we focus on the action we must take in this step: humbly asking, practicing spiritual principles, and getting out of God's way. The results of the Seventh Step may not materialize immediately, but they will in time.

- Do I believe that my Higher Power will remove my shortcomings or grant me freedom from the compulsion to act on them?
  Do I believe that I'll be a better person as a result of working this step?

- How does my faith in the God of my understanding become stronger as a result of working this step?

Trust and faith alone can never carry us through a lifetime of working this step; we need to practice patience, too. Even if it's been a long time since we started asking for the removal of a shortcoming, we still must be patient. Maybe, in fact, impatience is one of our shortcomings. We can look at the times when we have to wait as gifts—the times when we most need to practice the principle of patience. After all, one of the surest ways we progress is by rising up over the barriers we run into on our spiritual path.

- Where have I had opportunities for growth lately? What did I make of them?

Finally, we need to maintain our awareness of the principle of humility, more than any other, as we work this step. It's fairly easy to see if we're approaching this step with humility by asking ourselves a few questions:

- Do I believe that only my Higher Power can remove my shortcomings? Or have I been trying to do it myself?

- Have I become impatient that my shortcomings haven't been removed right away, as soon as I asked? Or am I confident that they will be removed in God's time?

- Has my sense of perspective been out of proportion lately? Have I begun thinking of myself as more significant or more powerful than I really am?

Moving on

At this point, we may wonder how we're supposed to be feeling. We've asked the God of our understanding to remove our shortcomings; we've faithfully practiced the principles of our program to the best of our ability; but we may still find ourselves acting out before we've had a chance to think, and always struggling with our defects. Sure, we're no longer using, and many of the outside circumstances of our lives have probably gotten better—our relationships are more stable, perhaps—but have we changed? Have we become better people?

In time, we'll find that God has worked in our lives. We may even be startled by the level of maturity or spirituality we've demonstrated in handling a situation that in years past would have had us acting *very* unspiritually. One day, we'll realize that some of the ways we used to act have become as alien as spiritual principles were when we first started practicing them. After such a revelation, we may begin thinking about the person we were when we first came to NA and how little we resemble that person now.

- Have there been times when I've been able to refrain from acting on a character defect and practice a spiritual principle instead? Do I recognize this as God working in my life?

- Which shortcomings have been removed from my life or diminished in their power over me?

- Why does the Seventh Step foster a sense of serenity?

We begin to live more spiritual lives. We stop thinking so much about what we're going to *get*, even from our recovery, and start looking at how we can contribute. The things we do to sustain and nourish our spirits become habits; we may even look forward to them. We find that we're free to choose how we want to look at any situation in our lives. We stop grumbling about small inconveniences as if they were major tragedies. We become able to hold up our heads with dignity and maintain our integrity, no matter what life presents us. As we begin to get more comfortable with our spiritual selves, our desire to heal our relationships will grow. We begin that process in Step Eight.

"We made a list of all persons we had harmed, and became willing to make amends to them all."

—Step Eight

To this point, the steps have focused mostly on repairing ourselves and our relationship with a God of our understanding. Beginning with the Eighth Step, we bring other people into the healing process—people we harmed in our addiction, people we harmed in our recovery, people we meant to harm, people we hurt by accident, people who are no longer in our lives, and people we expect to be close to for the rest of our lives.

The Eighth Step is about identifying the damage we caused. It doesn't matter whether we caused it because we were overtaken by rage, carelessness, or because we were afraid. It doesn't matter whether our actions were based in selfishness, arrogance, dishonesty, or any other defect. It doesn't even matter that we didn't intend to cause someone harm. All the damage we caused is material for the Eighth Step.

It may turn out that some of the harm we did can't be repaired. It may turn out that we, ourselves, can't directly make the repair. It may even turn out that we're not responsible for something we've placed on our Eighth Step list. Our sponsor will help us sort that out before we go on to the Ninth Step. For now, our task is only to identify who we harmed, and what the harm was, and become willing to make amends.

It's natural to wonder about the Ninth Step and how we will make our amends while we're working the Eighth Step. What we think about our amends is bound to influence our work in this step. We may need to get some common misconceptions out of our way before we can make our list.

It's wonderful that we've already begun repairing our relationships with some of the people in our lives. Our families are probably delighted that we're no longer using drugs. Some of the more overt damage we inflicted on others ceased as soon as we stopped using drugs. If we managed to keep our jobs or stay in school, we're probably already performing better in those places. We're no longer harming our co-workers or employers, our teachers or fellow students in certain ways. But is that enough?

We have probably heard people in meetings emphasizing that "amends" means to change, not just to say "I'm sorry"—that what really counts is the way we're treating people now. But this doesn't mean that formal apologies have gone out of fashion in NA. Direct, face-to-face verbal amends are extremely powerful, both as a means of spiritual growth for us and as a long-awaited comfort for the people to whom we make them. What our members are emphasizing is that we can't just offer people lame apologies and then go right back to doing what caused them harm in the first place.

Some of us may be feeling a bit weary at this point, especially if our sponsor had us do extensive writing on the first seven steps. We inventoried our behavior in Step Four, and we catalogued our character defects in Step Six; now we have to examine the same situations from yet another angle! It may seem as if we've examined our lives and our addiction in every possible way by the time we're done with these steps. Is all this really necessary? Aren't we just punishing ourselves by going over and over the same thing?

71

No, we're not. The Eighth Step is the beginning of a process that lets us feel equal to others. Instead of feeling shame and guilt, instead of feeling forever "less than," we become able to look people in the eye. We won't have to avoid anyone. We won't have to be afraid we'll be caught and punished for some neglected responsibility. We'll be free.

• Am I hesitating in any way about working the Eighth Step? Why?

Some of us go to the other extreme with this step: We can't wait to get right out there and "make everything okay," unaware that we may cause more harm. We blunder forward, confessing infidelities to our spouses and our friends. We sit our families down and make them listen to every detail of our addiction, confirming some of their worst fears about what we were doing out there and filling in some blanks that, until then, had been left mercifully empty. In a state of excitement, we give our children a speech about how we have a disease for which we're not responsible, how we love our recovery, and how wonderful life is going to be from then on, forgetting all the times before when we had made them so many empty promises. We stroll into our employer's office one day and announce that we're addicts, that we've embezzled a great deal of money through ingenious means, but that we're very sorry and we'll never ever do it again.

Though our own experiences with rushing out to make amends are probably not this extreme, we can surely grasp the point: If we try to make amends without our sponsor's guidance and without a plan, we can end up causing even more harm.

• Do I realize the need to slow down and consult my sponsor before making amends? Have I created more harm in any situation by rushing out to make amends before I was ready? What was the situation?

Some of us may still believe that we're just basically nice people who have never truly harmed anyone—except ourselves, that is. If we're truly stumped about who belongs on our amends list, or we have a vague idea that our family belongs there but we're not sure why, it could be that we're overlooking something or that our denial is still pretty thick. Sometimes we're just not able to see the truth about certain situations, even after many years in recovery. A suggestion that many of us have followed is that if we think of someone to whom we seem to owe amends, but we can't think of the situation that resulted in our owing amends, we put the name on the list anyway. Sometimes we'll think of the "why" later on. We should do the best we can with this step for now, contact our sponsor, and keep working on our recovery. As the saying goes, "more will be revealed." We just need to keep an open mind, so that when the knowledge comes we'll be prepared to accept it.

Last but not least, many of us delay starting this step because we aren't willing to make amends to certain people. We either resent them or we feel too afraid to ever imagine ourselves approaching them. We need to start this step and list these people even if we're not sure we'll ever be able to make the amends. If it's truly unsafe to make the amends, our sponsor will help us figure out how to handle the situation.

- List the resentments that are in the way of my willingness to make amends.

- Can I let these resentments go now? If not, can I muster the willingness to add these names to my list anyway, and worry about becoming willing later?

- Are there any people to whom I owe amends who may be a threat to my safety or about whom I'm truly concerned in some other way? What are my fears?

The People We Harmed and How We Harmed Them

Before we actually begin making our list, there's one final concept with which we must familiarize ourselves: the meaning of "harm" in this step. We need to strive to understand all the ways in which it is possible to cause harm so that our list can be thorough.

Certain types of harm are obvious. For instance, if we stole money or property from a person or a business, that's quite obviously a form of harm. In addition, most of us have no trouble recognizing physical or emotional abuse as a type of harm.

Then there are situations where we have no problem recognizing what we did as harmful, but may have difficulty identifying who, in particular, we harmed. For instance, we cheated on a test at school. Did this harm the instructor, we ask ourselves? Our fellow students? Ourselves? The students who came after us and had to pay the price of our instructor's mistrust because of our dishonesty? The answer to this example is that all of these people were harmed, even if only indirectly. They belong on our Eighth Step list.

Finally, we get to the deeper types of harm. These types of harm may be the most damaging, for they strike at the most vulnerable places in the human heart. For instance, we had a friend. The friendship was perhaps an old one, spanning many years. Emotions, trust, even personal identity—all these were engaged in the friendship we shared. This relationship really mattered to our friend, and to us as well. Then, without explanation, because of some real or imagined slight, we withdrew from the friendship and never tried to renew it. Losing a friend is painful enough without the added burden of not knowing why, but many of us inflicted just this type of harm on someone. We damaged that person's sense of trust, and it may have taken many years to heal. A variation on this is that we may have allowed someone to take the blame for a relationship ending, making the person feel unlovable, when in reality we had just grown tired of the relationship and were too lazy to maintain it.

There are many different ways we can inflict deep emotional harm: neglect, withdrawal, exploitation, manipulation, and humiliation, to name but a few. The "victims" and "nice people" among us may find that we made others feel inferior when we passed ourselves off as better than everyone else, projecting an attitude of moral superiority. The competent and self-sufficient among us may find names for the Eighth Step list by thinking about the people whose offers of help and gestures of support we rejected.

An additional struggle that many of us face when we identify types of harm arises from an automatic tendency to focus only on the time *before* we stopped using. It's a little easier for us to be rigorously honest about the harm we caused in our active addiction. We were using drugs, we were different people then. However, we have all caused harm during our recovery. (Remember, whether we intended to or not doesn't matter.) In fact, we've probably all caused harm to people with whom we share our recovery—other NA members. We may have gossiped about them, withdrawn from them, responded with insensitivity to their pain, interfered in a sponsorship relationship, tried to control a sponsee's behavior, behaved like an ingrate with a sponsor, stolen Seventh Tradition money, manipulated people by using our clean time as a source of credibility in a service argument, or sexually exploited a newcomer, to name a few relatively common examples. Most of us have an extremely hard time placing these situations on our Eighth Step list because the thought of making the amends makes us so uncomfortable. We hold ourselves accountable to a higher standard of behavior around NA, and we're sure that others expect more from us, also. The fact is that our fellow NA members are likely to be especially forgiving because they know what we're trying to do—but again, we should avoid worrying about the Ninth Step now.

Making Our List

The first thing to know is that this is not a list that we can keep in our heads. We need to put each name and what we did to harm the person down on paper. Once it's on paper, it's hard to forget anyone or go back into denial about an amends we'd rather avoid. If for some reason we can't use paper, we can use a tape recorder or any other method our sponsor has agreed will help us get the most out of this step.

When we're ready to begin our list, we sit down, recall all we've learned about harm, and start writing. Some names are going to spring to mind immediately. Others may come to mind as we think about the types of harm we have caused. We absolutely need to go back through our Fourth Step and search out any information we can extract from that.

We should include every name and situation we think of even if we're relatively, but not entirely, sure that our sponsor is going to tell us we don't owe any amends in that particular situation. It's almost always better to delete names than to try to recall names we should have added, but didn't, when we're going over the list with our sponsor. In addition, there may be times when we remember an incident in which we caused harm, but not the names of the people involved. We can at least list the incident.

Putting ourselves on the list may seem awkward to some of us. We may have been informed in our early recovery that making amends to ourselves was a self-centered idea, that we needed to stop thinking about ourselves all the time and start thinking about the people we had harmed. Then, the whole notion of making amends to ourselves may have been confusing. Some of us probably thought that making amends

74

should involve "rewarding" ourselves for staying clean or some other accomplishment. We may have tried to do this by buying ourselves things we couldn't afford, or by indulging other compulsions. In reality, the way we make amends to ourselves is by stopping irresponsible or destructive behavior. We need to identify the ways we've created our own problems—that is, harmed ourselves—through our inability to accept personal responsibility. Then, when we add ourselves to the list, we can list the harm we caused to our finances, our self-image, our health, etc.

There is also a delicate situation that many of us have faced: What if we've harmed our sponsor, and he or she doesn't know about the harm, and will likely find out when we go over the list? In this situation, we should consult another member whose recovery we respect, perhaps our sponsor's sponsor.

• List the people I've harmed and the specific ways I harmed each one.

Becoming Willing

Now that we have our list, or have added new names to the list we've been keeping since our first time through the Eighth Step, it's time to get willing to make amends. In order to become willing, we have to know at least a little about what "making amends" involves. Earlier in this guide, we talked about the need to do more than just change our behavior, but some of us may be afraid that we just aren't capable of changing. We're sincere. We want to refrain from ever repeating the same behavior again, but we think about the times when we've made promises before. Aren't we subject to doing the same thing again? This is when we have to really believe in our recovery. No matter how long we've been clean and the wrongs for which we're making amends, we have to have faith that the God of our understanding will give us the strength and the ability to change. For some of the amends we owe, we'll find that we're willing as soon as we put the name on our list. For others, the willingness may not come so easily.

• Why is saying "I'm sorry" alone not sufficient to repair the damage I've caused?

• Why is only changing my behavior not sufficient to repair the damage I've caused?

It's very rare that we don't owe at least some financial amends, whether they're to people from whom we stole, people who lent us money we never paid back, businesses, or lending institutions. We know that making the amends is going to deprive us of money we'd rather keep for ourselves. It may take time for us to appreciate the profound internal freedom that comes from discharging such debts, and thus gain the willingness to make these amends. It may help to ask our Higher Power to give us the willingness to make these amends.

• Do I have financial amends that I don't want to make?
What would my life be like if I had already made these amends?

Some of our amends may be to people who also harmed us. These are usually the amends we have the most difficulty becoming willing to make. It seems like every time we think about these amends, we get so angry thinking about what *they* did to *us* that we forget all about making amends. But our recovery calls on us to practice the spiritual principle of forgiveness. Through prayer and any additional help we need to seek out, we *can* find it within ourselves to forgive the people who have also harmed us.

- Do I owe amends to people who have also harmed me?
  What have I done to become willing to make these amends?

Amends that we can't ever see ourselves making may also be on our list. Maybe we're so unwilling that we don't even want to try praying for willingness; we can't imagine having any compassion for the people to whom we owe these amends. In this case, we just need to leave these amends on our list. We don't have to make all our amends in one day or in any set amount of time. It may take some time to become willing to make some amends. Every time we look at our Eighth Step list, we should ask ourselves if we've become willing to make *this* amends yet. If not, we can keep checking periodically.

Spiritual Principles

In the Eighth Step, we will focus on honesty, courage, willingness, and compassion. To practice the principle of honesty in the Eighth Step, we need to draw on our experience in the previous steps. We've admitted the nature of our problem—addiction—and affirmed the solution to that problem. This was an act of honesty. We've taken a searching and fearless moral inventory of ourselves; doing so exercised our newfound honesty. Extracting the nature of our wrongs from within the fabric of our personalities took our honesty to an even deeper level. So we have some experience separating our part in things from what others may have done. That's the level of honesty we'll need to call on in Step Eight. We have to forget about resentments, blaming others, believing we were innocent victims, and any other justification for the harm we caused. We simply need to *put it on the list*!

- How is determining the exact nature of my wrongs valuable in the Eighth Step?
  Why is it so essential that I'm clear about my responsibility?

- What are some examples of my experience with honesty from the previous steps?
  How will I translate that experience into this step?

To practice the principle of courage in the Eighth Step, we have to put ourselves in God's care. We can't restrict our list to only those amends that we think will turn out okay. We have to believe that our Higher Power will provide us with the fortitude, the humility, the inner strength, or whatever we need to get through any amends. Whether we need to face someone and we're afraid of how we'll feel, or we need to accept the consequences of a crime for which we are sought, we'll be able to handle it with the help of our Higher Power.

- What are some examples of my experience with courage from the previous steps? How will I translate that experience into this step?

We've already talked a great deal about willingness in this step, especially becoming willing to make amends. But we need a certain amount of willingness to work this step that has nothing to do with making amends. First of all, we need the willingness to make our list. No matter what we're feeling about adding a certain name to the list, we need to become willing to add it. We also need the willingness to practice the other spiritual principles connected to this step.

- Are there any names I haven't yet added to my list? Am I willing to add them now? Have I completed my list?

- What are some of the things I've done to increase my willingness?

- How do I feel about having to pray for willingness?

Developing a compassionate spirit becomes possible at this stage in our recovery. Before we did the work involved in the previous steps, we were too caught up in resentment, blame, and self-pity to think about others. Along with our ability to think of ourselves as ordinary human beings, we begin to see that others are doing the best they can with their humanness, too. We know we are subject to periodic doubts and insecurities about ourselves, and so are others. We know we are likely to speak before thinking, and so are others. We realize that they regret it as much as we do. We know we are prone to misreading situations and over or underreacting to them. As a result, when we see others act on a character defect today, we feel empathy rather than annoyance or anger, because we know what caused them to act as they did. Our hearts feel full when we think about how we share the same dreams, fears, passions, and faults as everyone else.

- Am I beginning to feel connected with others? Describe.

- Am I beginning to feel compassion and empathy for others? Describe.

Moving on

Discussing every single one of the amends on our list with our sponsor is essential. It doesn't matter how long we've been clean or how much experience with making amends we have. Every one of us is liable to misjudge a situation when working alone, but we often find that we can see things more clearly when we look at situations from another point of view. We need our sponsor's insight. We need our sponsor's encouragement. We need our sponsor's vision and hope. It's amazing how much a simple discussion with our sponsor can do to help us tap into the quiet strength that lives in each one of us. When we've stripped away the distracting influences and have exposed that solid core of serenity, humility, and forgiveness, we're ready for the Ninth Step.

"We made direct amends to such people wherever possible, except when to do so would injure them or others."

—Step Nine

We hear over and over in NA that the steps are written in order for a reason: Each step provides the spiritual preparation we'll need for the following steps. Nowhere is this more apparent than in the Ninth Step. We would never in a million years have been able to sit down with the people we've harmed and make direct amends without the spiritual preparation we got from the previous steps. If we had not done the work of admitting our own limitations, we wouldn't now have a foundation on which to stand while we make our amends. If we had not developed a relationship with a God of our understanding, we wouldn't now have the faith and trust we need to work Step Nine. If we had not done our Fourth and Fifth Steps, we would probably still be so confused about our personal responsibility, we might not even know for what we're making amends. If we hadn't developed humility in the Sixth and Seventh Steps, we'd probably approach our amends with self-righteousness or anger and wind up doing more damage. The willingness we gained through our acceptance of personal responsibility made it possible for us to make our Eighth Step list. That list was our practical preparation for working the Ninth Step.

The final preparations we're about to do in this step, before we actually make our amends, are mostly to strengthen what is already a part of us. The level at which we are able to practice the principle of forgiveness, the depth of insight we have, and the amount of self-awareness we are able to maintain throughout the amends process will depend on our previous experience with the steps and how much effort we're willing to put into our recovery.

- How has my work on the previous eight steps prepared me to work the Ninth Step?

- How does honesty help in working this step?

- How does humility help in working this step?

Amends

The Ninth Step is not a step that can be neatly contained within a particular time frame. We don't write our Eighth Step list and then resolutely start making amends, crossing off "completed" ones like we would items on a shopping list. In fact, many of our amends will never be "finished"; our efforts will go on throughout our recovery. For instance, if we owe our families amends, we will spend the rest of our lives practicing the spiritual principles that will bring real change to the way we treat people. There may be one day when we sit our families down and make a commitment to treat them differently than we have in the past, but that won't be the end of our amends. Each day that we make an effort to refrain from hurting our families and try to practice loving behavior with them is a day when we've continued our amends to our families.

Even such relatively concrete amends as paying a past-due debt aren't likely to be done once and for all when the debt is paid off. Living our Ninth Step requires that we try not to incur new debts that we can't pay. On a deeper level, we may need to look at the varieties of debt we incur—for instance, taking favor after favor from friends but never reciprocating, or overextending the patience of people with whom we share responsibilities by not assuming our fair share. Avoiding such liabilities in the future is just as much a part of our amends process as making regular payments on past-due debts.

- What does "making amends" mean?

- Why does making amends mean that I have to do more than say "I'm sorry"?

- How is making amends a commitment to a continuous process of change?

Fears and Expectations

Making amends isn't always a nerve-wracking, joyless experience. Often, we will feel excited about the prospect of healing a relationship. We may find that we're happily anticipating the relief of having made an amends. For most of us, however, we will feel fearful about at least some of our amends. We may be afraid that if we make financial amends, we won't have enough for ourselves. We may be afraid of rejection, retaliation, or something else.

If we've never had any experience with the Ninth Step before, we're really venturing into the unknown. We're not sure how we're going to feel immediately before the amends, during the amends, and after the amends. We may feel wildly overconfident at one moment and then, the next moment, feel totally unable to go on with the Ninth Step. This is a time when it's very important to understand that the ways things *feel* is not necessarily the way things *are*. Just because we feel afraid doesn't mean there's truly something to fear. On the other hand, feeling excited and happy won't necessarily reflect the reality of making our amends. It's best to let go of all our expectations about how our amends will be received.

- What fears do I have about making amends? Am I worried that someone will take revenge or reject me?

- How does the Ninth Step require a new level of surrender to the program?

- What about financial amends? Do I have faith that the God of my understanding will ensure I have what I need even though I am sacrificing to make amends?

No matter how long we've been clean or how many times we've been through the steps, we're bound to have some fears and expectations as we begin a new step. This may be especially true if we have previous experience with a step. The Ninth Step, in particular, is likely to produce some ambivalence.

For instance, many of us may find ourselves thinking about our past experiences with making amends at this point. Some have probably been very positive. If we made amends to a loved one who was open to our gesture of conciliation, we probably came away with a wonderful feeling of hope and gratitude. We were hopeful that the relationship would keep on getting better, and we were grateful to be forgiven and have our amends accepted.

Believe it or not, such experiences may work against us in later amends. They can set us up to believe that all our amends should turn out so well, and then be crushed when they don't. Or we may recognize that such amends aren't going to be the norm, and dread to the point of delay making amends whose outcome we aren't sure will be so good. If we find ourselves hung up on projecting how our amends will turn out, we need to re-focus on the purpose of the Ninth Step.

The Ninth Step is meant to give a way to set right the damage we've caused in the past. Some of us keep in mind that three primary concepts are associated with making amends: resolution, restoration, and restitution. Resolution implies that to find an answer to the problem, we must lay to rest what was previously plaguing or disturbing us in some way. Restoration means to bring back to its former state something that had been damaged. This can be a relationship or a quality that used to exist in a relationship, such as trust. We can perhaps restore our reputations if they were good at some point in the past. Restitution is very similar to restoration, but in relating it to the Ninth Step, we can think of it as the act of returning something—material or more abstract—to its rightful owner. Our sponsor can help us explore each of these concepts so that we can gain perspective on the nature of making amends and stay focused on what we're supposed to be doing. It's only through the process that we realize many of the benefits associated with the Ninth Step. The ones that we may be aware of first are a sense of freedom, or an absence of guilt and shame. It may take some time in recovery or experience with several amends for us to appreciate some of the spiritual rewards of the Ninth Step: a more consistent awareness of the feelings of others and the effect of our behavior on others, a sense of joy that we were able to heal a long-standing hurt, an ability to be more loving and accepting of the people around us.

- What other fears or expectations do I have about my amends?
- Why doesn't it matter how my amends are received?
  What does this have to do with the spiritual purpose of the Ninth Step?
- How can I use other addicts, my sponsor, and my Higher Power as sources of strength in this process?

Amends—Direct and Indirect

We in NA tend to think it's best to make direct, face-to-face amends, and indeed, this step says we should do so wherever possible. But direct amends are not the only way to make amends, and in some cases they may be the worst way.

Before we provide some examples, it is very important to note that these are only examples. This guide is not meant to take the place of a sponsor in going over each amends with a sponsee and working together to decide what's best.

Some situations are more complicated than they appear at first glance. We may think the solution is obvious, but we should always take the time for further reflection. For instance, there may be a situation where the person or people we've harmed are not aware of what we did, and learning what we did might possibly harm them more. We may have some friends, relatives, or an employer who were unaware of our addiction. To tell them might harm them. Our sponsor will help us look at our motives for wanting to tell people about our addiction. Do they need to know? What good purpose will be served by sharing such information? What damage could such information do?

But what if this same situation was complicated by our theft of some money from our friends? And what if someone else was accused of taking the money? Wouldn't we then need to tell about our addiction, along with admitting the theft and paying the money back? Possibly, but perhaps not. Each of these kinds of situations needs to be taken on an individual basis. Again, our sponsor will help us decide how best to handle each one. In our discussion with our sponsor, if we are open-minded, we're sure to think about these kinds of situations in ways we haven't thought about them before. We may see how what we first thought was the obvious method of making amends may not be right after all. It's very helpful to prepare for this discussion by listing all the circumstances for these difficult amends so that it will be right in front of us when we talk to our sponsor.

- Which names on my Eighth Step list are complicated by circumstances like the ones above? What were the specific circumstances?

A problem that presents difficulty for many of us is that we owe amends that will likely result in us losing our jobs, going to jail, or some other serious consequence. For instance, if we turn ourselves in for a crime we committed, we may indeed go to jail. So what effect would that have on our lives? Would we lose our job? Would that compromise anyone's security besides our own—say, our family's? On the other hand, if we are a fugitive from justice, what effect might a sudden arrest have on our lives and our families? It is probably best in such a situation to seek legal counsel and explore our options. No matter what, we need to somehow accept the consequences of our behavior, but we should bear in mind that our families might very well be represented in the part of this step that says, "except when to do so would injure them or others." We'll have to evaluate these situations very carefully. With our sponsor's guidance, we'll explore *how* to make amends.

- Do I owe any amends that might have serious consequences if I made them? What are they?

Another circumstance when we wouldn't be able to make direct amends, although not because of the possibility of further injury, would be when a person to whom we owe amends is dead. This is very common around NA—so much so that our members have developed a variety of creative ways of dealing with such situations. Our members have even managed to make sure that amends of this nature do more than discharge our own sense of shame. Some have made financial donations in the name of the person to whom we owed amends. Some have taken on a task that was something that person cared about. Some have made restitution to the person's children, who may have their own spot on our Eighth Step list. The ways we might deal with such a situation are only limited by our imagination and level of willingness. We might be surprised at how effective an "indirect" amends can be in situations like this. Many of us strive to make the amends as directly as possible by visiting the person's grave or other meaningful place and perhaps reading a letter or simply speaking to the person's memory or spirit. Again, our response to these situations will be determined by the nature of the harm we inflicted, our spiritual beliefs, and, of course, our sponsor's guidance.

- Do I owe amends to anyone who is dead? What was special about that person that I might be able to use in planning my amends?

We've been emphasizing the need to check each and every amends with our sponsor before proceeding. While that's important, there's no need for us to become mindless robots, afraid to think for ourselves or act without asking our sponsor about it. Many of our members have had the experience of running into a person from our past whom we had not put on our Eighth Step list, but who might belong there. Sometimes the amends owed are so clear, we would be foolish not to avail ourselves of such a lucky coincidence. Other times, we may run into a person and experience very uncomfortable feelings but not know what's causing them. If this happens, it's better to take the relationship through the Fourth and Fifth Step process in order to gain more clarity about it. In any event, we should never consider our Eighth Step list "closed." Chances are we'll be adding new names to it throughout our lives.

What about people we can't find? Should we go ahead and make indirect amends to them, too? Perhaps, although many of our members have had the experience of running across someone we thought we'd never be able to find, usually in a location in which we'd never expect to find them. We can certainly draw the conclusion that a Higher Power is at work when such coincidences happen, but even if not, we certainly shouldn't ignore the opportunity to make direct amends.

If we can't find someone on our amends list, we may want to wait. We should continue making every effort to find the person, we should make an effort not to cause the same type of harm to someone else, and we should remain willing. A spirit of willingness can often serve the purpose of the amends when we cannot make the actual amends.

After considering the complications involved in making indirect amends, it may seem as though making direct amends is easy, or at least more straightforward. We did something that hurt someone. We need to apologize and repair the harm. That's it, right?

Not very often, if ever. As mentioned earlier, the amends process isn't one that has a distinct beginning and end. We often begin making amends, in one sense, as soon as we get clean. Most of the time we immediately amend some of our behavior. This part of the amends process—the one in which we change ourselves—goes on long after we've spoken directly to someone we harmed.

• What behavior do I need to amend?

What about those direct amends, the ones we make when we sit someone down, acknowledge and accept responsibility for the harm we caused, and accept whatever response we get? These are the amends that may strike fear into our hearts. We imagine ourselves sitting before one of the people on our amends list, humbly and sincerely admitting our wrong, then just as humbly and sincerely offering to repair the wrong, only to have the person respond, "It can never be repaired. What you did was too awful," or, "Forget it. I'll never forgive you."

In truth, a situation like the above is exactly what we most fear, because we're afraid of having our faith in the process destroyed. We've taken an incredible risk by allowing ourselves to believe in a Higher Power, in ourselves, in the possibility of recovery. Our worst nightmare is that the damage can't be repaired, that we're such horrible people that we can't be forgiven. It may comfort us to know that many recovering addicts have received a negative reaction from someone they were making amends to, and not only have they not let it get them down, but they've received the same spiritual benefits from making the amends as they would have if it had been received with love and forgiveness.

Sometimes, when our attempts at making amends are received so negatively, we do find that we need to take additional steps so that we can feel we've attained some resolution. Our Basic Text tells us that "contacting someone who is still hurting from the burn of our misdeeds can be dangerous." It can also be unproductive, especially in the case of family members and close friends. Contacting people we've harmed before they've had the chance to cool off may cause them to respond very angrily to us, when after a bit more time they would have reacted quite differently. If we've approached such a person too soon, we may want to wait until some time has passed and try again.

Sometimes, however, no matter how well we've prepared or how sincere our amends, the person simply won't accept our amends. If we encounter this situation, we need to realize that there is a point at which our responsibility ends. If someone is determined to nurse a grudge against us for the rest of their lives, it may be that the best we can do is wish the person well and consider the amends made. If we have difficulty coping with feelings that arise in the wake of such an amends, our sponsor will help us find a way of coming to terms with the amends. Perhaps, in certain situations, we may be better off making indirect amends, or it may feel like our amends are more "complete" if we take some other action that restores or repairs a situation. For instance, we've tried to make amends to a former employer from whom we stole money. He or she doesn't want to hear our amends and doesn't want our money. We may find that we can resolve the situation and make restitution by referring customers to the person's business or, if it's possible, somehow anonymously paying back the money we stole.

We need to remember that making amends is part of our personal recovery program. It's true that we make amends because we owe them, but we also need to recognize the spiritual growth inherent in the process of making amends. First, we recognize and accept the harm we caused. As it says in It Works: *How and Why*, this "shocks us out of our self-obsession." Because self-obsession and self-centered fear are the parts of our disease that most strongly affect our spirituality, alleviating and diminishing those parts of our disease will surely cause our recovery to flourish. Second, approaching the person we harmed directly and acknowledging the harm we caused is an enormous step on our spiritual journey *no matter how the amends are received*. The fact that we went ahead with something that required such a great deal of humility was proof, in fact, that we had attained some measure of humility. Finally, after making our amends, we are left with a sense of freedom. We are no longer burdened with the weight of unfinished business and a sense of shame about the harm we caused. It is gone. Our spirits soar.

- Am I spiritually prepared for making any difficult amends and dealing with the results?
- What have I done to prepare myself?

Forgiveness

The spiritual growth we get from making direct amends often depends on how much we put into our spiritual preparation. We start with getting rid of any beliefs we have that may be causing us to hesitate or might inhibit our ability to approach our amends with humility, acceptance, and faith.

Something that seems to be a problem for many of us is that we often owe amends to people who have also harmed us. This may be a parent or other relative who abused us, a friend who let us down somehow, an employer who didn't treat us fairly, and so on. We've done a lot of work in the previous steps to separate what they did to us from what we did to them. We know exactly what our part in these situations was, and we know why we are making amends. As we prepare to make direct, face-to-face amends, we need to be perfectly clear that we are making amends for our part in these conflicts. We're not making amends to coerce or manipulate a reciprocal amends. We're not responsible for cleaning up anything not on our side of the street. Keeping this in mind throughout our amends will help us keep focused on our purpose no matter how our amends are received and whether or not we receive amends in return for harm done to us.

Sometimes, though, the wrong done to us was so extreme that it's better to postpone making our amends until a later time. For instance, many of us were emotionally, physically, or sexually abused as children by an older relative. Though we had no part in that situation and owe no amends because of it, we may have stolen money or caused physical or property damage to the relative at some other time. So we owe amends for the theft, physical harm, or vandalism. The question that arises in this situation is not *whether* to make amends, but when and how. It may take a long time before we are ready to make an appropriate amends, and that's okay. We wait, and we work with our sponsor.

We need to try to forgive the people who have harmed us before we make amends to them. We don't want to sit down with someone with whom we're furious and try to make amends. Our attitude will be apparent, no matter how much we try to hide it. Amends are a time when it's not usually very productive to "act as if."

There's a big difference between situations when we were harmed against our will and situations in which our behavior contributed to the way we were treated. For many of our amends, when we're angry at someone who treated us badly, we need to ask ourselves if anything we did could have caused them to treat us as they did. For instance, we may be enraged at our parents for not trusting us to go out on a weekend—to an NA dance!—but when we think about how many times we lied before about where we were going and always used drugs wherever we went, it may help us see that our parents can't help treating us with mistrust and that we may have to spend more time earning their trust. Or we may have been selfish and withdrawn with some of our friends day after day, week after week; then, when we needed them and they weren't available, we became angry and resentful. Reminding ourselves that we engineered much of our own misery may help us forgive those who hurt us.

Another way we may find forgiveness for those who hurt us is by getting out of ourselves and thinking about what other people's lives are like. Maybe the people who hurt us did so because they had problems that made them less sensitive to the needs of others. Maybe our sponsor didn't return our phone calls for a week because his youngest child was in jail. Maybe our best friend told us our relationship was unhealthy and we should get out of it—immediately following her own divorce. Maybe our employer didn't praise our work because he was worried about being able to meet payroll that week. We usually feel petty and small when we find out that a person we resented had some painful problem. Maybe we can be more forgiving and loving if we just assume from the start that most people's intentions are good and that if someone is unkind to us, it may be because he or she is in a lot of pain and very distracted by it.

First and foremost, preparing ourselves spiritually to make amends requires that we tap into our Higher Power's strength and love. Contemplating a loving God's forgiveness of the times when we hurt people will help us approach people with an attitude of love and forgiveness. Using our Higher Power as a sort of protective force will ensure that negative reactions to our amends don't cause us to lose hope. We can center ourselves by praying and meditating before each amends.

- Do I owe amends to people who have also harmed me?

- Have I forgiven them all? Which ones have I not forgiven yet?
  Have I tried all of the above ways of generating a spirit of forgiveness?
  What does my sponsor say about it?

Making Amends

Now we're ready to make our amends. We've discussed each person or institution on our Eighth Step list with our sponsor and made a plan for how we would go about making each amends. We've talked to the God of our understanding, and we've prayed for the willingness, serenity, courage, and wisdom to go through with our amends.

Now we need to follow through with our amends. We need to continue amending our behavior, and we need to keep whatever commitments we've made to the people on our amends list.

This is where it can get difficult. When we first make an amends, we're usually feeling as if we could float away on a cloud of freedom. We feel a heightened sense of self-respect and the initial euphoria that comes along with the disappearance of a large chunk of remorse. We feel like good people, like we're on equal footing with the rest of humanity. This feeling is extremely powerful, and if it's our first time feeling it, it might seem like more than we can handle.

We shouldn't worry. The feelings won't be so intense for long, though there will be some permanent change in our feelings about ourselves. After the first glow of making amends fades, we'll face the truly challenging part of making amends: the follow-through. For instance, a year after we approach a lending institution to which we owe money and promise to pay back a certain amount every month, we may not find it "spiritually inspiring" to hand over a portion of every hard-earned paycheck, especially if we're going to be making the same payment for several more years. Asking ourselves one simple question should help us continue with our amends: How free do we want to be? To continue with all aspects of our recovery, making amends included, makes our freedom grow day by day.

- Are there amends with which I'm having trouble following through? What am I doing to recommit myself to making these amends?

It is not necessarily a comforting and comfortable process to make amends. The steps aren't designed to make us happy and comfortable without also making us grow. The fear, the risk, and the feeling of vulnerability that come with making amends may be so uncomfortable for us that the memory keeps us from repeating the behavior that led to us having to make amends. We hear often around NA that "it gets better." "It" is us—we get better. We become better people. We become less willing to engage in destructive behavior because we are aware of the cost in human misery, both our own and that of those around us. Our self-centeredness is replaced by an awareness of other people and concern about their lives. Where we were indifferent, we begin to care. Where we were selfish, we begin to be selfless. Where we were angry, we begin to be forgiving.

Our love and tolerance also extend to ourselves. We explored some of the issues surrounding making amends to ourselves in Step Eight; now it's time to recognize how we've already begun making amends to ourselves and perhaps make some plans to continue or take on some new things. We began making amends to ourselves for our addiction when we stopped using drugs and started working the steps. Just these two acts will go a long way toward healing the damage we did to our own spirits. We may have to do some other things to heal the damage we did to our bodies and minds. There are many ways we can begin taking care of our physical health, from diet to exercise to medical treatment. Whatever ways we choose will need to fit our personal needs and desires. The damage we did to our minds may be healed in some measure by pursuing knowledge in the future. A return to school, or just learning something new, will help us repair years of mental neglect.

- What are my immediate plans for making amends to myself?
  Do I have any long-range goals that might also fit as amends to myself?
  What are they? What can I do to follow through?

Spiritual Principles

In the Ninth Step, we will focus on humility, love, and forgiveness. The humility we've gained in this step has resulted from getting a good look at the damage we did to others and accepting responsibility for it. We acknowledge to ourselves, "Yes, this is what I've done. I'm responsible for the harm I caused *and* for making it right." We may have been led to this awareness by the experience of having someone tearfully tell us how much we hurt them. We may have found ourselves on the receiving end of some hurt we had inflicted on someone else, and been so jarred by such an experience that we were able to see on a deeper level how we hurt people. Then again, it may have been only the process of the previous steps, coupled with the experience of making amends, that led us to experience increased humility.

- Have I accepted responsibility for the harm I caused and for repairing that harm?

- What experiences have I had that led me to see the harm I caused more clearly?
  How has that contributed to an increase in my humility?

It becomes much easier to practice the spiritual principle of love in Step Nine, though we've probably been working on practicing it throughout our recovery. By this time, we've eliminated many of the destructive views and feelings we had, making room for love in our lives. As we become filled with love, we find ourselves compelled to share it by nurturing our relationships and building new ones and by selflessly sharing our recovery, our time, our resources, and, above all, ourselves with those in need.

- How am I giving of myself or being of service to others?

As we experience being forgiven, we begin to see the value in extending that to others. This motivates us to practice the spiritual principle of forgiveness as much as possible. Recognizing our own humanness gives us the capacity to forgive others and not be as judgmental as we have been in the past. It becomes second nature for us to give other people the benefit of the doubt. We no longer suspect vile motives and sneaky conspiracies are at play in every situation over which we don't have full control. We're aware that we usually mean well, and so extend that belief to others. When someone does harm us, we're aware that holding resentments only serves to rob us of our own peace and serenity, so we tend to forgive sooner rather than later.

- What are the benefits to me of practicing the principle of forgiveness?
  What are some situations in which I've been able to practice this principle?

- For what have I forgiven myself?

Moving on

Many of us find it helpful to reflect on our amends after making each one. Some of us do this by writing about how it felt to make the amends and what we learned from the experience.

- How did it feel to make this amends? What did I learn from it?

"Freedom" seems to be the word that most clearly describes the essence of Step Nine. It seems to sum up the relief from guilt and shame, the lessening of our obsession with ourselves, and the increased ability to appreciate what's going on around us as it's happening. We start being less consumed with ourselves, more able to be fully present in all our relationships. We begin to be able to just be in a roomful of people without trying to control the room or dominate every conversation. We start thinking of our past, specifically our addiction, as a gold mine of experience to share with people we're trying to help in recovery, instead of as a period of darkness we want to forget about. We stop thinking about our lives in terms of what we don't have and begin to appreciate the gifts we receive every day. We know that to keep this feeling of freedom, we'll need to keep applying what we've learned in the previous steps. Step Ten gives us the means to do that.

"We continued to take personal inventory and when we were wrong promptly admitted it."

—Step Ten

Through working the first nine steps, our lives have changed dramatically—way beyond what we expected when we first came to Narcotics Anonymous. We've become more honest, humble, and concerned about others, less fearful, selfish, and resentful. But even such profound changes aren't guaranteed to be permanent. Because we have the disease of addiction, we can always return to what we were before. Recovery has a price—it demands our vigilance. We have to continue doing all the things we have been doing for our recovery so far. We have to continue to be honest, to have trust and faith, to pay attention to our actions and reactions, and to assess how those are working for us or against us. We also have to pay attention to how our actions affect others, and when the effects are negative or harmful, promptly step forward and take responsibility for the harm caused and for repairing it. In short, we have to continue to take personal inventory and promptly admit our wrongs.

As you can see, the Tenth Step has us repeat much of the work we did in Steps Four through Nine, though in a much-shortened format. The format suggested in this guide is one that covers in a general way the elements of a personal inventory. Some of us may find that we need to add questions that focus on specific areas that are affecting our individual recovery to the questions already in this guide. We may find some additional areas upon which to focus from IP #9, *Living the Program*. Our sponsor may have specific direction for us on this point. As noted before, this guide is meant to be a starting point, not the final word on any of the steps.

- Why is a Tenth Step necessary?

- What is the purpose of continuing to take personal inventory?

- How can my sponsor help me?

Feeling versus Doing

We use Step Ten to create and maintain a continuous awareness of what we're feeling, thinking, and, even more importantly, what we're *doing*. Before we begin a regular pattern of personal inventory, it's imperative that we understand what we are assessing. It won't do much good to make a list of our feelings without tying them to the actions that they generate or fail to generate. We may often be feeling very badly though behaving very well, or vice versa.

For instance, an NA member walks into her home group. "How are you?" someone asks. "Terrible," she replies. Of course, this member is referring to the way she feels. She can't possibly be referring to what she's doing, because she is behaving very well indeed: She's going to a meeting, honestly expressing how she feels, and reaching out to another member who will be supportive.

On the other hand, we may be busy indulging our impulses and acting on character defects. On the surface, we may feel very good. It usually takes a while before we notice the emptiness that goes along with living this way. We're avoiding the work that will help us stay clean. We're indulging our impulses, and taking the easy way out. And we know where this will take us!

The Tenth Step will keep us aware of ourselves so we don't end up going to either extreme. We don't have to beat ourselves up because we feel badly. We can instead focus on the positive action we're taking. It may even turn out that by shifting our focus this way, we'll wind up feeling better, too. Staying aware of what we're doing helps us see patterns of destruction long before they become entrenched, so we don't wind up feeling good at the cost of what's good for us.

We as addicts also tend to make judgments about what we are feeling. Anything that feels bad we immediately want to stop. We often don't take into account that the way we're feeling makes perfect sense when we consider the circumstances.

For instance, many of us have problems being angry. We don't like the way it feels. We judge it, concluding we have no right to feel that way, and then we do our very best to suppress our angry feelings. Yet, we may be experiencing a situation that would make anyone angry. Perhaps we're in a relationship with someone who constantly fails to treat us with respect. Perhaps we've been passed over for several well-deserved promotions at work. Our response to these situations is anger. We've been treated poorly—of course we're angry. Now comes the moment when our recovery can propel us forward into greater self-respect or our disease can drag us down into a thick fog of depression and resentment.

It all has to do with how we respond to our anger. If we scream and curse and throw things, we'll destroy any possibility of making our relationship or job situation better. If we do nothing and bury our feelings of anger, we'll become depressed and resentful, and that won't improve our situation either. But if we take positive action aimed at improving the situation, it may get better; at the very least, we'll know when it's time to leave and be able to do so without regrets.

Sometimes the only thing we need to do with our feelings is feel them. We don't need to react to them. For instance, if we've lost someone, we are going to feel sorrow. Our sorrow may go on for a long time. It will lift when we've grieved sufficiently. We can't afford to let our sorrow drag us down to the point where we can't go on with our lives, but we should expect to be affected. We may be easily distracted or have a hard time participating in activities that are supposed to be enjoyable. We need to strike a balance between being in denial of our feelings and letting them overwhelm us; we don't want to go to either extreme. This seems like a simple concept—almost as if it could go without saying—but many of our members share that it takes years of recovery before we're able to achieve a balance most of the time.

So the Tenth Step grants us the freedom to feel our feelings by helping us see the difference between feeling and doing.

• Are there times in my life when I am confused about the difference between my feelings and my actions? Expand on this.

Right and Wrong

The Tenth Step tells us that we have to promptly admit when we're wrong. The step seems to assume that we know when we're wrong, but the fact is that most of us don't—at least not right away. It takes the consistent practice of taking a personal inventory for us to become proficient at figuring out when we're wrong.

Let's face it. When we were new in recovery, we had been at odds with the rest of the world for some time. As the Basic Text says, our "living skills were reduced to the animal level." We didn't know how to communicate with others well. We began to learn in recovery, but in the process, we made a lot of mistakes. Many of us went through a period of time when we became very rigid about the values we had developed in recovery. We applied that rigidity not only to ourselves, but to everyone around us. We thought it was principled and correct to confront those whose behavior was "unacceptable." In truth, it was our behavior that was unacceptable. We were self-righteous and overbearing. We were wrong.

Or some of us, after years of serving as a doormat for everyone to walk across, decided our recovery required that we become assertive. But we went too far. We demanded that everyone treat us perfectly all the time. No one could have a bad day and fail to return our phone call. No one was allowed to be emotionally unavailable to us for any length of time. We angrily demanded perfect service at the places we did business. We weren't being assertive. We were being immature and belligerent. We were wrong.

We can even end up being wrong if someone hurts us. How? Say our sponsor says something very hurtful to us. Instead of taking it up with our sponsor, we talk to ten or twelve of our closest friends at the next three meetings we go to. Before the week is through, half our local NA community is talking about the rotten thing so-and-so said to one of his sponsees—and that's if the story stayed as it was originally! So the situation started out with us having done no wrong, but ended up with us being responsible for damaging our sponsor's reputation in the program—the place where he needs, as much as we do, to be allowed to make mistakes and recover at his own pace.

• Have there been some times in my recovery when I've been wrong and not been aware of it until later? What were they?

• How do my wrongs affect my own life? Others' lives?

It's hard enough to figure out when we're wrong; admitting our wrongs can be even more challenging. Just like in the Ninth Step, we have to be careful that we aren't doing more damage by making the admission.

For instance, many of us realize we've hurt someone close to us—perhaps because the person stopped speaking to us—but aren't quite sure what we said or did wrong. Rather than taking the time to reflect on what we might have done, or ask the person, we decide we'll just cover all eventualities and make a blanket admission. We approach the person and say, "Please forgive me for anything I've ever, in all the time we've known each other, done to offend you or hurt you."

The Tenth Step requires that we take the time for personal reflection for instances just like this. Chances are that if we think about when the person's attitude toward us changed, and think about our behavior immediately preceding that change, we'll know what we did wrong. It might be painful or embarrassing to think about; it definitely takes effort, but so do all the steps. Laziness is a character defect like any other, and we can't afford to act on it. Then again, if we're truly stumped, if we just can't pinpoint anything we might have said or done that was harmful, there's nothing wrong with approaching the person and saying we've noticed that he or she seems to be angry or upset with us, that we care about our relationship with that person and want to hear what he or she has to say. Most of us are afraid of what we'll hear in a situation like this, but we can't let our fear stop us from working Step Ten.

There's another way we can render our admission of wrong completely ineffective: admit we're wrong and then immediately point out what the other person did first that made us act as we did. For instance, say one of our children used poor manners, so we yelled at her and called her a name. Now when we admit we were wrong, if we tell our child that her behavior made us act the way we did, we've just delivered a message that justified our first wrong, thus making ourselves doubly wrong.

Unlike the process contained in Steps Four through Nine, when we go through events from the past, Step Ten is designed to keep us current. We don't want to let unresolved wrongs pile up. We need to try our very best to stay abreast of what we're doing. Most of our work will be done by making constant adjustments to our outlook. If we find ourselves becoming negative and complaining all the time, we might want to spend some time thinking about the things for which we are grateful. We need to pay attention to the way we react when we've done something wrong. Is it our first impulse to make an excuse? Are we claiming to be victims of someone's negative influence—or of our disease? All excuses aside, we are responsible for what we do. It may very well be that our character defects got the better of us, but that doesn't excuse our behavior. We need to accept responsibility, and continue to be willing to have our shortcomings removed.

- "When we were wrong promptly admitted it"—what does this mean to me?

- Have there been times in my recovery when I've made situations worse by talking to someone before I should have or blaming my behavior on someone else? What were they?

- How does promptly admitting my wrongs help me change my behavior?

Step Ten points out the need to continue taking personal inventory and seems to assert that we do this solely to find out when we're wrong. But how can we identify the times we're wrong unless we also have times we're right as a basis for comparison? Identifying the times we do things right and forming personal values are as much a part of personal inventory as identifying our liabilities. Most of us have a very difficult time with the concept of being right. We think of the times we vigorously defended an opinion because we just knew we were right, but in light of our recovery, we've come to understand that trampling over others in a discussion makes us wrong. Or we think of our personal values. We know they're right for us, but if we began insisting that others live them, we would no longer be right, but self-righteous. So how do we get comfortable with being right? First and foremost, by working the Sixth and Seventh Steps so that our character defects don't turn our positive acts into negative acts. Then, we have to realize that it will probably take some time, and some trial and error, before we are completely comfortable in our new lives in recovery.

- Have there been situations in my recovery in which I felt uncomfortable about acknowledging something I had done well? Describe.

How often Should We Take a Personal Inventory?

It Works: How and Why tells us that while our goal is to maintain continuous awareness of ourselves throughout each day, it's very helpful to sit down at the end of each day and "work" this step. We need the consistency of doing something every day for it to become a habit and to internalize the spiritual principles of the activity. As we stay clean and our days of continuous abstinence turn into weeks and months and years, we'll find that taking a personal inventory has become second nature. We'll find that keeping track of our spiritual fitness comes naturally, without our having to think too much about it. We'll notice right away when we're headed in a direction we don't want to go or about to engage in a behavior that's sure to cause harm. We become able to correct it. So, the frequency of our formal efforts to take personal inventory may depend on our experience with recovery. In the beginning, some of us sat down at the beginning of our day, at the end of our day, or even both times, and went through IP #9, *Living the Program*, or something similar and "took our spiritual temperature." The point is that we want to keep at it until it becomes a habit, until it's second nature to continuously monitor our recovery and our spiritual state, notice when we're going off course right away, and work to change it.

- Why is it important to continue to take personal inventory until it becomes second nature?

A Personal Inventory

The following questions address the general areas we want to look at in a personal inventory. There may be times when our sponsor wants us to do an inventory on a specific area of our lives, such as romantic relationships or our patterns at work, or our sponsor may have specific questions to add to this. We should always consult our sponsor on any step work we're doing.

- Have I reaffirmed my faith in a loving, caring God today?
- Have I sought out the guidance of my Higher Power today? How?
- What have I done to be of service to God and the people around me?
- Has God given me anything to be grateful for today?
- Do I believe that my Higher Power can show me how to live and better align myself with the will of that power?
- Do I see any "old patterns" in my life today? If so, which ones?
- Have I been resentful, selfish, dishonest, or afraid?
- Have I set myself up for disappointment?
- Have I been kind and loving toward all?
- Have I been worrying about yesterday or tomorrow?
- Did I allow myself to become obsessed about anything?
- Have I allowed myself to become too hungry, angry, lonely, or tired?
- Am I taking myself too seriously in any area of my life?
- Do I suffer from any physical, mental, or spiritual problems?
- Have I kept something to myself that I should have discussed with my sponsor?
- Did I have any extreme feelings today? What were they and why did I have them?
- What are the problem areas in my life today?
- Which defects played a part in my life today? How?
- Was there fear in my life today?
- What did I do today that I wish I hadn't done?
- What didn't I do today that I wish I had done?
- Am I willing to change?
- Has there been conflict in any of my relationships today? What?
- Am I maintaining personal integrity in my relations with others?
- Have I harmed myself or others, either directly or indirectly, today? How?
- Do I owe any apologies or amends?
- Where was I wrong? If I could do it over again, what would I do differently? How might I do better next time?

- Did I stay clean today?

- Was I good to myself today?

- What were the feelings I had today?
  How did I use them to choose principle-centered action?

- What did I do to be of service to others today?

- What have I done today about which I feel positive?

- What has given me satisfaction today?

- What did I do today that I want to be sure I repeat?

- Did I go to a meeting or talk to another recovering addict today?

- What do I have to be grateful for today?

Spiritual Principles

In the Tenth Step, we will focus on self-discipline, honesty, and integrity. Self-discipline is essential to our recovery. When we were using, we were self-seeking and self-absorbed. We always took the easy way out, giving in to our impulses, ignoring any opportunity for personal growth. If there was anything in our lives that required a regular commitment, chances are that we only followed through if it wasn't too hard, if it didn't get in the way of our self-indulgence, or if we happened to feel like it.

The self-discipline of recovery calls on us to do certain things regardless of how we feel. We need to go to meetings regularly even if we're tired, busy at work, having fun, or filled with despair; we need to go regularly even when—especially when—we're feeling hostile toward the demands that recovery makes on us. We go to meetings, call our sponsor, and work with others because we have decided we want recovery in NA, and those things are the actions that will help assure our continued recovery. Sometimes we're enthusiastic about these activities. Sometimes it takes every bit of willingness we possess to continue with them. Sometimes they become so woven into our daily existence, we're hardly aware that we're doing them.

- Why is the principle of self-discipline necessary in this step?

- How can practicing the principle of self-discipline in this step affect my entire recovery?

The principle of honesty originates in Step One, and is brought to fruition in Step Ten. We are usually nothing less than amazed at the range and depth of our honesty by this point in our recovery. Where before we may have had honest hindsight, able to see our true motives long after a situation was over, we are now able to be honest with ourselves, about ourselves, while the situation is still occurring.

- How does being aware of my wrongs (self-honesty) help me change my behavior?

The principle of integrity can be quite complex, but it is integrity, more than anything else, that commands our ability to practice other principles. In fact, integrity is knowing which principles we need to practice in a given situation, and in what measure. For instance, we're standing outside a meeting one night, and happen to be part of a group that begins gossiping about someone else in the program. Let's say they're discussing the affair our best friend's spouse is having, and we know it to be true because we heard it from our best friend the previous night. Knowing what to do in this situation will probably take every ounce of integrity we possess. So which spiritual principles do we need in this situation? Honesty? Tolerance? Respect? Restraint? It's probably our first impulse to rush in, condemning the gossip because we know how much it would hurt our friend to have such private matters discussed publicly. But by doing so, we may confirm the gossip's truth and so hurt our friend more, or we may end up self-righteously humiliating the people involved in the gossip. Most of the time it isn't necessary to prove we have integrity by confronting a situation we don't approve of. There are a couple of things we could do in this situation. We could either change the subject or we could excuse ourselves and walk away. Either of these choices would send a subtle message about our feelings and, at the same time, allow us to be true to our own principles and spare our friend as much as possible.

- What situations in my recovery have called on me to practice the principle of integrity? How have I responded? Which times have I felt good about my response, and which times have I not?

Moving on

One of the most wonderful things about the Tenth Step is that the more we work it, the less we'll need the second half of it. In other words, we won't find ourselves in the wrong as often. When we come to recovery, most of us have never been able to have any kind of long-term relationship, certainly not any in which we resolved our conflicts in a healthy and mutually respectful way. Some of us had raging fights with people and, once they were over, never spoke of the underlying problems that caused the fights. Some of us went to another extreme, never disagreeing at all with the people who were supposed to be our closest friends and relatives. It seemed easier to keep our distance than to risk creating a conflict that we may then have had to deal with. Finally, some of us just walked away from any relationship in which conflict arose. It didn't matter how much we were hurting the other person; it seemed easier than working through a problem and building a stronger relationship.

The Tenth Step makes it possible for us to have long-term relationships—and we need to have long-term relationships, especially in NA. After all, we depend on each other for our very lives. Many of us feel deeply connected to the people who came to NA when we did and have stayed around. We've done service work with one another, shared apartments with one another, married one another, and sometimes divorced one another. We've celebrated milestones in each other's lives: births, graduations, buying homes, promotions, and recovery anniversaries. We've mourned losses together, and we've comforted one another through the painful times in life. We've touched each other's lives and formed a shared history. We are a community.

Along with learning to admit when we're wrong comes a freedom that is unlike any we've ever experienced before. It becomes so much more natural for us to admit when we're wrong that we wonder why we ever found it so terrifying. Perhaps because we felt so "less than" in so many ways, an admission of a mistake felt like we were revealing our deepest secret: our inferiority. But when we found out through working the steps that we weren't inferior at all, that we had just as much value as anyone else, it no longer seemed so crushing to admit we were wrong. We began to feel whole.

- How does the Tenth Step help me live in the present?
- What am I doing differently as a result of working Step Ten?

Working the Tenth Step makes it possible for us to achieve more balance and harmony in our lives. We find that we're happy and serene much more often than not. Feeling out of sorts becomes so rare that, when it does happen, it's a signal that something is wrong. We can readily identify the cause of our discomfort by taking a personal inventory.

The personal freedom that has been building since we began working the steps yields an increase in our choices and options. We have total freedom to create any kind of life we want for ourselves. We begin to look for the meaning and purpose in our lives. We ask ourselves if the lifestyle we have chosen helps the still-suffering addict or makes the world a better place in some other way. What we are searching for, we'll find in the Eleventh Step.

*"We sought through prayer
and meditation to improve our
conscious contact with God
as we understood Him,
praying only for knowledge
of His will for us and the power
to carry that out."*

—Step Eleven

Step Eleven says that we already have a conscious contact with the God of our understanding, and that the task before us now is to improve that contact. We began to develop our conscious awareness of a Higher Power in Step Two, learned to trust that Power for guidance in Step Three, and relied on that Power many times for many other reasons in the process of working through the steps. Each time we called upon our Higher Power for help, we improved our relationship with our Higher Power. Step Eleven recognizes that reaching out to the God of our understanding, referred to most simply as prayer, is one of the most effective means for building a relationship with God. The other means put forth in this step is meditation. In this step, we will need to explore our own concepts of prayer and meditation, and make sure they reflect our spiritual path.

Our Own Spiritual Path

The Eleventh Step allows us the opportunity to find our own spiritual path, or further refine our path if we've already embarked on one. The steps we take toward finding or refining our path, and the way we walk down it, will depend to a large degree on the culture in which we live, previous experiences with spirituality, and what best suits our personal nature.

Our spirituality has been developing since we first came to NA. We are constantly changing, and so is our spirituality. New territory, new people, and new situations have their effect on us, and our spirituality needs to respond.

Exploring our spirituality in the Eleventh Step is a wonderful and illuminating experience. We will be exposed to many new ideas, and we'll find that many of these new ideas come directly from our own knowledge of spiritual matters. Because we've developed a frame of reference about spirituality in the previous ten steps, we find that our insight has grown along with our capacity to comprehend new information about ourselves and our world. Spiritual exploration is wide open, and we will learn and find personal truths both in our concentrated efforts to understand more and in the most mundane details of our lives.

Many of us find that when we get to NA, we really need to "change Gods." Some of us believed in something we vaguely referred to as "God," but we didn't really understand anything about it except that it seemed to be out to get us. We probably did some work in Steps Two and Three aimed at uncovering unhealthy ideas about our Higher Power, and then we tried to form some new ideas that allowed for a loving, caring Higher Power. For many of us, simply believing that we had a Higher Power that cared about us as individuals was enough to get us through the following steps. We didn't feel any need to develop our ideas any further.

But our ideas were developing anyway, even without our conscious effort. Each specific experience with working the steps provided us with clues about the nature of our

Higher Power. We sensed truths about our Higher Power rather than understanding them intellectually. The moment we sat down with our sponsor to share our Fifth Step, many of us were suddenly filled with a quiet certainty that we could trust our sponsor, trust this process, and go forward; this was a moment in which many of us felt the presence of our Higher Power. This, along with the work we did in Steps Eight and Nine, implanted in many of us a growing awareness of our Higher Power's will for us.

- What experiences have I had with the previous steps or elsewhere in life that gave me some inkling of what my Higher Power is like?
  What did I come to understand about my Higher Power from those experiences?

- What qualities does my Higher Power have? Can I use those qualities for myself—can I experience their transformative power in my life?

- How has my understanding of a Higher Power changed since coming to NA?

These clues about the nature of our Higher Power are perhaps the primary factor in determining our spiritual path. Many of us have found that the spiritual path of our childhood doesn't mesh with the truths we are finding within the steps. For instance, if we sense that God is vast and open, and the spirituality we have been exposed to in the past suggested that God was confined and confining, we're probably not going to return to our earlier path. If we sense that our Higher Power cares in a very personal and individual way about each one of us, a belief system that presents a distant, unknowable, alien force may not work for us.

While some need to take a new path, others have found that just the opposite is true: that what we are discovering in the steps can be explored in more depth through the spiritual path of our childhood. It's possible that, through our step work, we've healed resentments we may have held against religious institutions, and as a result are able to return to those institutions with an open mind. For others, the religion of our childhood was little more than a place to hang out, a community to which we had a sentimental connection. In recovery, we begin to see how we can use our religion as our personal spiritual path.

It bears emphasizing that we should never confuse religion with spirituality. In NA, they are not the same thing at all. Narcotics Anonymous itself is not a religion. It offers a set of spiritual principles, and uses a concept referred to as "God," a "Higher Power," or a "Power greater than ourselves" for members to use as a path out of active addiction. The spiritual principles and the concept of a Higher Power can go along with a member's personal spiritual path that he or she follows outside of NA, or those principles and the concept of a Higher Power can serve as a spiritual path all by themselves. It's up to each member.

Some of us get to this point, and we just don't know. The institutions we've been involved with in the past hold no answers, but we can't think of anything that sounds like a better idea. For those with this experience, this is the point at which we embark on one of the most important journeys in our lives: the search for a way to understand a

Higher Power. In this process, we are likely to visit every place that has anything to do with spirituality that's available in our community. We're also likely to read a great number of books concerned with spirituality and personal growth, and talk to a great number of people. We may commit for a time to any number of practices before settling on one—or we may never really settle on any one practice permanently. *It Works* mentions that many of our members adopt an "eclectic approach" to spirituality. If this applies to us, it's important to know that doing this is okay and will serve the spiritual needs of recovery just fine.

- Do I have a specific spiritual path?

- What are the differences between religion and spirituality?

- What have I done to explore my own spirituality?

As we explore our spiritual path, and perhaps pick up and discard various spiritual practices, some of us are troubled by what seems to be an inherent bias in NA's steps and traditions when God is referred to as having a male gender. Even more painful, some of us may feel that we don't have much support within our local NA community for our spiritual choices and exploration. It's important for us to understand that the language of NA's recovery literature is not meant to determine a member's spirituality. It's also important for us to understand that we as addicts have character defects, and sometimes some of our members will act on theirs by ridiculing someone else's spiritual path. They may even quote NA recovery literature to "support" such ridicule. Again, NA itself has no "official" or "approved" spiritual path, and any member who claims otherwise is, quite simply, wrong. We mention this here because we believe it's very important for all of our members to know what's true and not true about NA when working the Eleventh Step. It can be a dangerous time. If members follow a spiritual path, and feel unwelcome in NA because of it, their recovery can be in jeopardy. We as members have a duty to encourage the spiritual explorations of other members, and we who are exploring need to know that we can look wherever we want for our spirituality without threatening our membership in NA.

- Have I encountered any prejudice in Narcotics Anonymous while exploring my spirituality? How did that make me feel? What have I done to adhere to my beliefs?

It's essential that we don't let our spiritual path take us away from the fellowship. Our Basic Text reminds us that "it is easy to float back out the door on a cloud of religious zeal and forget that we are addicts with an incurable disease." We need to always remember that we need Narcotics Anonymous in order to deal with our addiction. Anything else we add to our lives can enhance their quality, but nothing can take the place of NA recovery. As long as we continue practicing the basics of recovery—such as going to meetings regularly, staying in contact with our sponsor, and working with newcomers—we shouldn't have to worry about drifting away.

- No matter what spiritual path I am following, am I still keeping up my involvement with NA?

- How does my involvement in NA complement my spiritual journey?

- How does my spiritual path contribute to my recovery?

Prayer and Meditation

Members of NA often describe prayer as talking to God, and meditation as listening to God. This description has been part of the collective wisdom of NA for a long time because it captures the distinct meanings of prayer and meditation so well. We are building a relationship with our Higher Power, and we need to have a dialogue with that Power, not merely a monologue aimed in its direction.

Prayer *is* talking to our Higher Power, though not always in the form of actual speech. We worked on developing a form of prayer that felt right to us in the Second Step. We may find by now that we've further refined our approach to prayer to fit with our spiritual path. One of the forms of prayer in which virtually every NA member engages is the closing or opening prayer said at most NA meetings. Ultimately, the manner in which we pray is up to us as individuals.

How often should we pray? Many of us set aside a specific time in our day—the beginning is fairly common—to pray. These prayers usually involve asking our Higher Power for another day clean or, as we will explore more fully later in this chapter, knowledge of God's will for us. When we communicate with our Higher Power at the end of our day, it is usually to express gratitude. Many of us try to incorporate prayer throughout our day. It is very good practice to pray regularly. It helps us form a habit of communicating with our Higher Power that may save our recovery some day.

- How do I pray?

- How do I feel about praying?

- When do I usually pray? When I am hurting? When I want something? Regularly?

- How is it helpful to use spontaneous prayer throughout the day?

- How does prayer help me put things in perspective?

If this is our first experience with the Eleventh Step, we may be surprised to learn we've already been meditating, and doing so on a regular basis. Each time we stand as a community at a meeting and observe a moment of silence, we are meditating.

It is from such beginnings that we go on to build a pattern of regular meditation. There are many different ways we can go about meditating, but its usual goal is to quiet the mind so that we can gain understanding and knowledge from our Higher Power. We try to minimize distractions so that we can concentrate on knowledge arising from our own spiritual connection. We try to be open to receiving this knowledge. It's essential that we understand that such knowledge is not necessarily, or even usually, immediate. It builds in us gradually as we continue to practice regular prayer and meditation. It comes to us as a quiet sureness of our decisions and a lessening of the chaos that used to accompany all our thoughts.

- How do I meditate?

- When do I meditate?

- How do I feel about meditating?

- If I have been meditating consistently for some time, in what ways have I seen changes in myself or my life as a result of meditating?

Conscious Contact

To many of us, "conscious contact" sounds like something very mysterious, implying some kind of cosmic union with God. But it's really very simple. It just means that we have a conscious awareness of our link to a Higher Power. We notice the presence of that Power, and see some of the ways it works in our life. There are so many ways our members have experienced the presence of a loving God: when we experience something in nature, such as a forest or an ocean; through the unconditional love of our sponsor or other NA members; through the feeling of being anchored during difficult times; through feelings of peace and warmth; through a coincidence that later on we see as having led to some great good; through the simple fact of our recovery in NA; through our ability to listen to others at a meeting; and countless other means. The point is that we are looking, and we are willing to acknowledge that our Higher Power is active in our lives.

- In what circumstances do I notice the presence of my Higher Power? What do I feel?

- What am I doing to improve my conscious contact with the God of my understanding?

God's Will

The knowledge that has been building in us as we've prayed and meditated is the essence of God's will for us. The whole purpose of praying and meditating is to seek knowledge of a Higher Power's will for us and, of course, the power to carry it out. But the first thing to do is to identify God's purpose for our lives.

It takes a large amount of open-mindedness to begin to understand God's will for us. Many of us find that it is easier to identify what is *not* God's will for us than what is. This is absolutely fine; in fact, this is a great starting point that can lead us to more specific knowledge of God's will for us. First of all, and obviously, it is *not* God's will for us to relapse. We can extend this simple fact to conclude that acting in ways that might lead us to relapse are also *not* God's will for us. We don't need to become overly analytical about this and start questioning whether our daily routines could possibly lead to us relapsing; it's really much easier than that. We use all of the knowledge about ourselves and our patterns that we gained from the work we did in Steps Four through Nine, and we try our very best to avoid destructive patterns. We'll discover that we no longer have the luxury of consciously acting out. We can't deal with a situation by thinking, "Oh, I'll just be manipulative this one time, and then I'll write about it later, work with my sponsor, and make amends." If we do such a thing, we're not only on very dangerous ground, we're making a conscious and deliberate decision to go against God's will. There will be many, many times when we act on defects unconsciously. It is our consciousness and willingness to be deliberately destructive in this situation that are the real cause for concern.

In the Third Step, we explored the fine line that divides humble and honest pursuit of our goals from subtle manipulation and forced results. Now, with the experience we have gained in the intervening steps, we are much better equipped to spot that line and stay on the right side of it. As we go after the things we want, we need to continuously gauge our distance from that line. For instance, we may decide we want to be in a romantic relationship. There's nothing wrong with that, provided we are spiritually motivated and keep track of the line between God's will and self-will. If we lie to make ourselves seem more attractive, or become chameleons, we're acting on self-will. If we honestly express who we are, we're more likely to be pursuing God's will. If we're trying to change our potential partner in a relationship into something he or she is not, we're acting on self-will. If, on the other hand, we've already determined what we want in a partner and the person we're seeing seems to be matching that vision without our intervention, we're probably living in God's will. *That's* how we tell whether a relationship is God's will for us or not. Or say we want a college education. Are we willing to cheat on a test to get it? Doing such a thing would turn an otherwise worthy goal into an act of self-will. The avoidance of acting on self-will is the primary reason we pray only for knowledge of God's will for us and the power to carry that out.

- What are some situations I can identify from my own life where I acted on self-will? What were the results?

- What are some situations I can identify from my own life where I tried to align my will with God's will? What were the results?

As it says in *It Works: How and Why*, "God's will for us is the ability to live with dignity, to love ourselves and others, to laugh, and to find great joy and beauty in our surroundings. Our most heartfelt longings and dreams for our lives are coming true. These priceless gifts are no longer beyond our reach. They are, in fact, the very essence of God's will for us." Our personal vision of God's will for us is revealed in how our lives might be if we were consistently living with purpose and dignity. For instance, it is a good expression of purpose to help others stay clean and find recovery. The individual ways we go about doing that—sponsorship, sharing with newcomers at meetings, carrying the message into institutions, working with professionals to develop programs that will lead addicts to NA—are our choice.

- What are some examples of how I live with purpose and dignity?

- What is my vision of God's will for me?

The Power to Carry that Out

In addition to praying for knowledge of God's will for us, we're also asking for the power to carry out that will. In this context, power doesn't refer only to forceful qualities. There are many different qualities we may need to carry out our Higher Power's will: humility, a sense of compassion, honesty, integrity, or an ability to persevere and the patience to wait for results over a long period. A strong sense of justice and an ability to be assertive might be what's called for in a certain situation. Sometimes eagerness is required, and other times only a sense of caution will do. Courage and fortitude are qualities that we will often be called upon to display. Sometimes the best quality to promote God's will is a sense of humor.

Most likely we will need all of these qualities at various times in our lives. When we pray for the power to carry out God's will for us, we probably won't know exactly what qualities we need. We have to trust that the ones we need will be provided. It may be tempting for us to demand from our Higher Power the things we think we need, but we usually can't see the "big picture" or the long-term effects of something that seems very reasonable at the moment.

- Why do we pray only for knowledge of God's will for us and the power to carry that out?

- How does humility apply to this?

Spiritual Principles

In the Eleventh Step, we will focus on commitment, humility, courage, and faith. We need to make a commitment to the practice of regular prayer and meditation. Many of us find that our first experiences with prayer and meditation have us feeling kind of silly. We glance around the room to see if anyone is looking, and wonder just what we're supposed to be feeling, anyway. As we continue with our commitment, this feeling will pass, as will the ensuing feelings of frustration when the results aren't what we expect, and the boredom that sets in when the things we're doing become routine. The point is that we need to continue, no matter how we feel about it. The long-term results of peace of mind and a deeper relationship with our Higher Power are worth waiting for.

- How do I show my commitment to working the Eleventh Step and to my recovery?

- Have I prayed and meditated today?

The often-heard warning to "Be careful what you pray for!" captures the kind of humility we need to practice in this step. We simply need to acknowledge that we don't always know what's best for us—or for anyone else. That's why we ask for knowledge of *God's* will for us.

- Have I ever prayed for a specific thing and then wished I didn't have it after all? Expand on this.

There's nothing that requires as much courage as trying to live according to our Higher Power's will when there's frequent pressure not to. Not everyone in our lives will be delighted that we've chosen to live our lives in a spiritual way. We may have family members who are used to us living according to *their* will and want us to continue. Our growth threatens them.

Or say we're with some friends who are gossiping. Our efforts to live the program have resulted in us becoming uncomfortable with participating in gossip, yet we don't want to be self-righteous and start moralizing with our friends. Merely refraining from participating in something like this requires courage. We may lose some friends as we grow spiritually.

Almost all of us face some situation in life where we are either being asked to participate in something that is morally reprehensible or just keep quiet about it and allow it to happen. It may be that the truly courageous course of action is to protest loudly, and doing so may have severe consequences for us. What we do at such a time is a defining moment, and may very well affect the choices we make for the rest of our lives.

- Have I ever been faced with a situation that required me to stand up for my beliefs at some personal cost? How did I respond? What were the results?

The principle of faith will help us to practice the principle of courage and live our lives with integrity. We need not be so afraid of losing friends or having relationships change or even having our lives profoundly affected because we know that we're being cared for. We have faith that if we have to let go of old friends because what they're doing is unhealthy for our spiritual development, we'll form new relationships with people whose values we share. Basically, we need to have faith that we'll be given the power to carry out our Higher Power's will.

- Have I, so far, been given what I need? What have I received?

Moving on

Our practices in this step show up in every area of our lives. From the regular practice of meditation, we may notice that we are able to listen more attentively to what others have to say in meetings. We have some experience with quieting our minds and so are able to do so in many places. We no longer find ourselves so consumed with planning what we'll say when it's our turn that we are unable to listen to others.

We begin to be satisfied with our lives. We no longer feel such an urgency to control things. We're focused on a higher purpose instead of on ourselves. Our regrets begin to disappear. Our active addiction no longer seems like such a tragedy and a waste as we see how we can use that experience to serve a higher purpose: carrying the message to the addict who still suffers. In Step Twelve, we will explore some ways of doing that, and see how practicing the principles of recovery is essential to such an effort.

"Having had a spiritual awakening as a result of these steps, we tried to carry this message to addicts, and to practice these principles in all our affairs."

—Step Twelve

If we've made it to this point, we've had a spiritual awakening. Though the nature of our awakening is as individual and personal as our spiritual path, the similarities in our experiences are striking. Almost without exception, our members speak of feeling free, of feeling more lighthearted more of the time, of caring more about others, and of the ever-increasing ability to step outside ourselves and participate fully in life. The way this looks to others is astonishing. People who knew us when we were in our active addiction, often appearing withdrawn and angry, tell us that we're different people. Indeed, many of us feel as if we've begun a second life. We know the importance of remembering where we came from, so we make an effort not to forget, but the way we lived and the things that motivated us seem increasingly bizarre the longer we stay clean.

The change in us didn't happen overnight. It happened slowly and gradually as we worked the steps. Our spirits awakened a bit at a time. It became increasingly more natural for us to practice spiritual principles and increasingly more uncomfortable to act out on character defects. Notwithstanding the powerful, one-of-a-kind experiences some of us have had, we've all slowly and painstakingly built a relationship with a Power greater than ourselves. That power, whether it's our own best and highest nature or a force outside ourselves, has become ours to tap into whenever we want. It guides our actions and provides inspiration for our continued growth.

- What is my overall experience as a result of working the steps?

- What has my spiritual awakening been like?

- What lasting changes have resulted from my spiritual awakening?

Each time we work through the Twelve Steps we will have a different experience. Subtleties of meaning for each of the spiritual principles will become apparent, and we will find that as our understanding grows, we are also growing in new ways and in new areas. The ways in which we are able to be honest, for instance, will expand along with our basic understanding of what it means to be honest. We will see how practicing the principle of honesty must first be applied to ourselves before we are able to be honest with others. We will see that honesty can be an expression of our personal integrity. As our understanding of the spiritual principles grows, so will the depth of our spiritual awakening.

- Which spiritual principles have been connected to which steps, for me, and how have those contributed to my spiritual awakening?

- What does the phrase "spiritual awakening" mean to me?

We Tried to Carry this Message

Many of us recall the first time we heard the words, "You never have to use again if you don't want to." For many of us, hearing this message was shocking. Perhaps we'd never thought in terms of "having" to use before, and were surprised to find out just how much truth that statement held. *Of course*, we thought, *using drugs ceased to be a choice for me a long time ago.* Although just hearing this message may or may not have resulted in us immediately getting clean, we still heard the message. Someone carried it to us.

Some of us had the experience of believing that we could stay clean in NA, but when it came to recovery, that seemed beyond us. Gaining a sense of self-respect, making friends, being able to carry ourselves out in the "real world" without it being obvious that we were addicts all seemed like more than we could actually expect from NA. The day we began to believe that this program could do more for us than just help us stay clean was a time we remember as a turning point in our recovery. What happened to give us that sense of hope was that someone gave us a reason to believe. Maybe it was someone sharing at a meeting with whom we identified in a very personal way. Maybe it was the cumulative effects of hearing many addicts share that recovery was possible. Maybe it was the unconditional love and quiet insistence of our sponsor that we could recover. In whichever way we heard it, it was the message, and someone carried it to us.

Some of us have the experience of staying clean for a long time and finding joy in recovery. Then we experience a tragedy. Maybe it's the breakup of a long-term committed relationship or the death of a loved one. Maybe it's the relapse and death of someone with whom we have been friends in NA. Maybe it's that we find ourselves destitute. Maybe it's simply that we've realized that other NA members aren't perfect, and so they're capable of hurting us. Because of whatever crisis we've experienced, we find that we've lost our faith. We no longer believe that NA holds the answer for us. The bargain we thought we had made—we'd stay clean and try to do the right thing and, consequently, our lives would be happy—had been breached, and we were left wondering about our purpose in life all over again. At some point, we began to believe again. Maybe someone who had been through the same crisis reached out to us and helped us through in a way no one else could have. Again, someone carried the message to us.

• What are the different ways in which I've experienced the message?

So the message can be broken down very simply. It is that we can stay clean, that we can recover, that there is hope. Recalling the times when we heard the message personally will provide part of the answer to why we should now carry the message, but there is more.

"We can only keep what we have by giving it away." This saying is perhaps the most powerful reason we can present for carrying the message. Many of us wonder, though, exactly how this concept works. It's simple, really. We reinforce our recovery by sharing it with others. When we tell someone that people who go to meetings regularly stay clean, we are more likely to apply that practice to our own recovery. When we tell someone that the answer is in the steps, we are more likely to look there ourselves. When we tell newcomers to get and use a sponsor, we are more likely to stay in touch with our own.

There are probably at least as many ways to carry the message as there are recovering addicts. Greeting a newcomer whom we met at the previous night's meeting and remembering his or her name is powerful and extraordinarily welcoming to an addict who feels alone. Opening a meeting makes sure there is a place for the message to be carried. Taking on a service position in any capacity helps keep NA itself going, and we can do a great deal of good if we approach our service to the fellowship in a caring, loving, and humble way. Sponsoring other addicts brings to life the therapeutic value of one addict helping another.

• What kind of service work am I doing to carry the message?

Sometimes it's challenging to carry the message. The person with whom we've decided to share the message seems unable to hear it. This can range from someone who keeps relapsing to someone who keeps choosing destructive behavior. It's tempting to think that our efforts are being wasted and we should just give up on such a person. Before we make such a decision, we should think about all the mitigating circumstances. Say we're sponsoring someone who just isn't following our direction. We've suggested a writing assignment, and we don't hear from the person again until a fresh crisis is brewing. We've shared, with all the enthusiasm we can summon, about our own experience with the situation the person is facing, explaining in great detail how our disease was present and how we used the steps to find recovery, but our sponsee keeps doing the same destructive thing over and over again. This can be very frustrating, but before we give up, we need to remember that our choice isn't *whether* to carry the message, but *how*.

We need to get our own egos out of the way. We don't get to take credit—or blame—for someone else's recovery. We simply present the message as positively as we can, and remain available to help when we're asked. We also need to remember that we can't possibly know what's going on in another person's mind or spirit. Our message may seem to be missing its mark, but perhaps the person just isn't ready to hear it today. It may be that the words we spoke will stay with a person for a long time and may resurface at exactly the right moment. If we think about it, we can all recall things we heard NA speakers say when we were new that we didn't understand at the time, but which rose up in our minds years later and gave us reason to hope or a solution to a problem we were experiencing. We *carry* the message, and we share it freely, but we cannot ever force another person to *get* the message. The principle that applies to our fellowship's public relations policy—attraction, not promotion—applies very well to our personal efforts to carry the message, too.

It may also be the case that we're not the best person to sponsor someone. Individuals have different needs and learn in different ways. Some people may thrive with one sponsor but not do well with someone who has a different sponsorship style. Some sponsors give a lot of writing assignments. Some are very insistent about their sponsees going to a certain number of meetings. Some are very "proactive," while others may simply respond to a sponsee's stated needs. No type is better or worse than any other. They're just different.

Another time we might find it very hard to carry the message is when we're not feeling very positive about life or recovery. It's probably our first impulse to go to a meeting and dump all our problems out so we can purge them from our own spirits. But NA meetings exist to provide a place to carry the message. Dumping our problems without tying them to recovery or trying to make it clear what the message is doesn't further the primary purpose of our groups. We can carry the message even if we just point out that we're having terrible problems but are not using over it and that we're attending a meeting and reaching out to work on our recovery. In most cases, though, the best way to carry the message is to focus on the newcomers in the room and tell them what's good about recovery in Narcotics Anonymous. We should also keep in mind that sometimes, no matter how long we've been clean, we need to *hear* the message, and if we sit quietly in a meeting, we have a good chance of doing so.

- What are some different ways of carrying the message?
  Which ones do I personally participate in?

- What is my personal style of sponsorship?

- What is the difference between attraction and promotion?

- What does it do for me to carry the message?

- How are the Fifth Tradition and the Twelfth Step tied together?

- What keeps me coming back and trusting the NA program?

- What is selfless service? How do I practice it?

To Addicts

Why does the Twelfth Step specify that we carry the message to addicts? Why did NA work for us when nothing else had? Almost every one of us had someone—a teacher, a counselor, a family member, a police officer—tell us that using drugs was killing us and destroying all we cared about, that if we just stayed away from our using friends and otherwise limited our access to drugs, we'd be able to change our lives. Most of us probably even agreed on some level, unless we were in complete denial. So why couldn't we find relief until we found Narcotics Anonymous? What did those other NA members have that made us believe recovery was possible?

In a word: credibility. We knew that they, who were just like us, had stopped using and found a new way to live. They didn't care what we had or didn't have. It even said in the readings we heard at the beginning of the meeting that it didn't matter what or how much we used. Most of us were grateful to find out that we qualified. We knew we'd suffered enough, but we wanted to be accepted. And we were. The addicts who were there for us when we first started coming to meetings made us feel welcome. They offered their phone numbers and encouraged us to call any time. But what we really found important was the identification. Members who had used just like we did shared their experience with getting clean. Members who knew from personal experience exactly how isolated and alone we felt seemed to know instinctively that a simple, loving hug was what we needed. It seemed as if the whole group knew exactly what we needed without us having to ask.

We often say to one another that we're fortunate to have this program; it gives us a way to cope with life on life's terms. After we stay clean for a time, we realize that the principles of Narcotics Anonymous are actually completely universal and could probably change the world if everyone practiced them. We may begin to wonder why we don't open up NA to all those who have any kind of problem. As we learned from our predecessors, having a single purpose is probably one of the most effective ways of ensuring that the opportunity will remain for an addict to find the identification he or she needs. If NA tried to be all things to all people, an addict might walk in, wanting only to know how to stop using drugs, and not be able to find anyone who knew.

- Why was an NA member able to reach me in a way that no one else ever had? Describe the experience.

- What is the therapeutic value of one addict helping another?

- Why is identification so important?

We can't be all things to all people; we shouldn't even try. This doesn't mean, however, that we can't share our recovery with others. In fact, we won't be able to help it. When we live a program, the results show up in every aspect of our lives.

Practicing these Principles in all Our Affairs

When we talk about practicing the principles of recovery in all our affairs, the key word is "practice." We just need to keep trying to apply spiritual principles to our lives, not be able to do it perfectly in every situation. The spiritual benefits we derive from working this step depend on our effort, not our success.

For instance, we try to practice the principle of compassion in every situation in our lives. It's probably relatively easy to practice the principle of compassion with a still-using addict who has just walked into her first NA meeting, no matter how belligerent or needy that newcomer is. But what about someone who has just returned from a relapse, or a multiple relapser? What if he walks in blaming NA for his relapse? What if she casually walks back into the rooms projecting an attitude that seems to take recovery for granted? What if it's someone we sponsored? We may find that practicing the principle of compassion doesn't come as easily as it used to. We don't *feel* compassionate toward the person, but we can still practice the principle of compassion. All we have to do is continue to carry the message—without conditions. Our sponsor can help us learn how to be compassionate without giving the impression that we think relapsing is okay. We can pray and meditate, asking our Higher Power to help us be compassionate.

This step calls upon us to practice principles in *all* our affairs. Many of us would like to separate our careers, our romantic relationships, or another area of our lives from this requirement because we're not sure we can get what we want if we have to practice spiritual principles. For instance, it may very well lead to apparent success and financial reward if we compromise our principles at work. We may be asked to meet a production deadline that results in profits for the company but produces an inferior product that could compromise the safety of the people who purchase it. So what do we do? We practice the spiritual principles of our recovery. There are probably many different choices about the specific action to take in response to our principles; the important thing is that we respond to our principles.

What about NA service? Strangely enough, some of us reserve NA service as the one place where we forget our principles. We cease giving people the benefit of the doubt in a service setting. We openly accuse others of hatching plots, and we say cruel things because we're not practicing the principle of kindness. We set up impossible processes for those we elect to do a job because we're not practicing the principle of trust. We become self-righteous, belligerent, and sarcastic. It's ironic that we seem to want to attack those whom we trust with our very lives in recovery meetings. We need to remember to practice spiritual principles in any meeting, whether service or recovery. Service gives us many opportunities to practice spiritual principles.

Knowing which spiritual principle to practice in any given situation is difficult, but it is usually the opposite of the character defect we would normally be acting out on. For instance, if we feel compelled to exert absolute control over a situation, we can practice the principle of trust. If we would usually be self-righteous in a certain situation, we can practice the principle of humility. If our first impulse is to withdraw and isolate, we can reach out instead. The work we did in the Seventh Step on finding the opposites of our character defects and the work we did at the beginning of this step on identifying the spiritual principles in the previous steps will give us some additional ideas about the principles we need to practice. Though most of us will wind up with very similar lists of spiritual principles, the attention we devote to certain ones will reflect our individual needs.

- How can I practice principles in the different areas of my life?
- When do I find it difficult to practice principles?
- Which spiritual principles do I have a particularly hard time practicing?

Spiritual Principles

Even in the step that asks us to practice spiritual principles, there are specific principles connected to the step itself. We will focus on unconditional love, selflessness, and steadfastness.

Practicing the principle of unconditional love in the Twelfth Step is essential. Nobody needs love without conditions more than a suffering addict. We don't ask anything of the people to whom we are trying to carry the message. We don't ask for money. We don't ask for gratitude. We don't even ask that they stay clean. We simply extend ourselves.

This doesn't mean we shouldn't take reasonable precautions. If we believe it isn't safe to bring a suffering addict to our home, we shouldn't do it. Twelfth Step calls should always be done with another NA member. Nor does practicing the principle of unconditional love require that we allow ourselves to be abused. Sometimes the best way of loving and helping is to stop enabling someone else to use.

- How am I practicing the principle of unconditional love with the addicts I am trying to help?

Why do we carry the message? Not to serve ourselves, even though we benefit. We carry the message to help others, to help them find freedom from their addiction and grow as individuals. If we have an attitude that the people we sponsor are somehow our possessions, that their lives would fall apart if we were not directing their every move, that most likely they wouldn't even be clean without us, then we've missed the point of the Twelfth Step. We don't expect recognition for the number of sponsees we have or for how well they're doing. We don't expect recognition for being of service. We do these things to accomplish something good.

It's a great paradox that selfless service becomes an expression of our deepest selves. Through our work in the previous steps, we have uncovered a self that cares more about allowing a Higher Power to work through us than it cares about recognition and glory. We have uncovered a self that cares more about principles than the exercise of our individual personalities. Just as our disease is often expressed in self-centeredness, our recovery is expressed beautifully as selfless service.

- What is my attitude about sponsorship? Do I encourage my sponsees to make their own decisions and grow as a result? Do I give advice, or do I share my experience?
- What is my attitude about service? Could NA survive without me?
- How am I practicing the principle of selflessness in my efforts to be of service?

Practicing the principle of steadfastness means we need to keep on trying to do our best. Even if we've had a setback and fallen short of our own expectations, we need to recommit ourselves to recovery. Steadfastness keeps a bad morning or a bad day from turning into a pattern that can lead to our relapse. This commitment ensures that we will keep practicing the principles of our program despite how we feel. Whether we're happy about it, bored with it, disgusted by it, or completely frustrated over it, we keep on trying to work a program.

- Am I committed to my recovery? What am I doing to maintain it?
- Do I practice spiritual principles regardless of how I feel?

Moving on

Before we get too excited about the prospect of being finished with the Twelve Steps, we should realize that we're not—finished, that is. Not only will we continue trying to practice the spiritual principles of all Twelve Steps, which many of us call "living the program," but we will formally revisit each of the steps, probably many times, throughout our lives. Some of us may immediately begin working through the steps again with the perspective that we've gained from our journey thus far. Others wait for a time or concentrate on certain aspects of the steps. However we do it, the point is that whenever we find ourselves powerless over our addiction, whenever more has been revealed about our shortcomings or people we've harmed, the steps are available as our path to recovery.

We should feel good about what we've done. We have, in many cases for the first time, followed a process all the way through. This is an amazing accomplishment, something about which we should be very proud. In fact, one of the rewards of working an NA program is finding that our self-esteem has grown a great deal.

We find ourselves joining society. We can do things that seemed beyond us before: exchanging hellos with a neighbor or the clerk at our local market, taking on positions of leadership in our communities, joining in social events with people who don't know we're addicts and not feeling "less than." In fact, we may have looked with contempt upon such things in the past because we felt we'd never be able to fit in, but now we know we can. We become approachable. People may even seek out our advice and counsel on professional matters.

When we think about where we've come from and what our recovery has brought to our lives, we can only be overwhelmed with gratitude. As it says in *It Works*, gratitude becomes the underlying force in all that we do. Our very lives can be an expression of our gratitude; it all depends on how we choose to live. Each one of us has something very special and unique to offer in gratitude.

How will I express my gratitude?